WITH ALL
HER MIND

WITH ALL HER MIND

A Call to the Intellectual Life

Edited by RACHEL BULMAN

Foreword by Tracey Rowland

WORD
on FIRE.

Published by Word on Fire, Park Ridge, IL 60068
© 2022 by Word on Fire Catholic Ministries
Printed in the United States of America
All rights reserved

Cover design, typesetting, and interior art direction
by Rozann Lee and Cassie Bielak

Except where otherwise indicated, Scripture quotations are from the
New Revised Standard Version Bible: Catholic Edition (copyright © 1989, 1993),
used by permission of the National Council of the Churches of Christ in the
United States of America. All rights reserved worldwide.

25 24 23 22   1 2 3 4

ISBN: 978-1-685780-15-9

Library of Congress Control Number: 2021922711

"'You shall love the Lord your God with all your heart, and with all your soul, and with all your mind.' This is the greatest and first commandment."

—MATT. 22:37–38

Mary treasured all these words and pondered them in her heart.

—LUKE 2:19

Contents

Foreword

Pope St. John Paul II coined the expression "the feminine genius." Without having made anything like an academic study of the concept, I have always assumed he derived the idea from Edith Stein. She thought that women have a capacity, one might say a "radar," for discerning the personal dimension of any issue. By "personal," I mean that women can usually see beyond the surface of human actions to the deeper motivating forces in play behind them. It is something like a finely tuned power of intuition.

I had a recent experience of this when having breakfast with the Ratzinger Prize winner Professor Hanna-Barbara Gerl-Falkovitz. The topic of conversation was Martin Heidegger. She remarked that because of his health, Heidegger was rejected by two seminaries. I knew that he had left a Jesuit seminary, but I had no idea of the reason for this. I assumed he left because he had lost his faith, or because he did not like the curriculum or spiritual regime, or some combination of these factors. Whatever the combination of factors, I had assumed that his departure from the Jesuits was his own choice. I had no idea that he had been rejected by the Jesuits and by diocesan officials. However, Professor Gerl-Falkovitz explained that Heidegger was a very short man with poor health, and she thought that these factors, along with being twice rejected as a seminarian, had an impact upon his philosophy.

My thoughts then turned to another conversation from some years earlier, indeed almost three decades ago now. Fr. Patrick Lynch, who had been a student at the University of Munich during the time of the Second Vatican Council, looked at me across a table at a café in Cambridge and asked, "You *do* understand that Vatican II was all about Heideggerizing Catholic theology?" In other words, whatever Pope John XXIII may have had in mind when he explained that his purpose for calling the council was to "open windows," the fact was that for many German scholars, the particular windows they wanted to open entailed an engagement with Heidegger. Just as one cause of World War I may have been Kaiser Wilhelm's bad relationship with his English mother, and one cause of World War II may have been Hitler's early failure as an artist, the rejection of Heidegger from two seminaries may have sent shock waves through twentieth-century philosophy and Catholic intellectual life. The capacity to identify such cause-and-effect relationships, or at least be sensitive to them, is something I associate with the feminine genius.

Each of the authors who have contributed to this collection has found inspiration in the idea of the feminine genius. Each contribution is unique, but taken as a mosaic, this book offers a window into the lives of significant Catholic scholarly women of our time. Some are young and single; others are juggling marriage, motherhood, and a professional life; and others have chosen the path of the evangelical counsels. All have signed up for frontline service in what the Australian poet James McAuley called the "wars of love." St. John Paul II called it the battle for the civilization of love.

My own experience is that the life of a Catholic scholar is never easy, but it is also never boring. It is, fundamentally, a vocation. It is never easy because one gets thrown into the center of the cosmic battle. Indeed, one often finds, as one of the contributors to this collection notes, that being on the payroll of the Church in no way guarantees a workplace where Christian principles prevail. Nominally Catholic institutions and agencies can be themselves bloody battlefields. The inverse side of this coin, however, is that the hotter the battle, the deeper the friendships that are forged, and the darker the nights of the soul, the more luminous the mornings of grace that arise from them. A central element of salvation history is that there is no glory without the cross—no Easter Sunday without a Good Friday.

Hans Urs von Balthasar understood this, as did his cofounder of the Community of St. John, the mystic Adrienne von Speyr, who had experiences of the stigmata over the Easter Triduum. Balthasar also suggested that the characters who surrounded Christ in the Gospels are "spiritual types" in the Church. In other words, different Apostles showcase different missions in the life of the Church. The scholarly vocation has always seemed to me to be a fusion of the missions of St. John and St. James. For a Catholic scholar, the contemplative side of St. John needs to combine with knowledge of the Catholic intellectual tradition and a disposition of filial fidelity in its transmission, typical of St. James. There also needs to be a Marian dimension—what Balthasar called *disponibilité*—the availability to serve and an openness to receiving the gifts of the Holy Spirit.

For there to be a "space" that makes this all possible—in other words, for there to be institutions that nurture Catholic intellectual life—there needs to be creative episcopal governance. Quite simply, we need bishops who understand the importance of the intellectual life and are prepared to support it politically, financially, and spiritually. This is part of what Balthasar called the Petrine mission.

Throughout this collection, a number of names are frequently cited as showcase examples of the feminine genius. Teresa of Avila and Thérèse of Lisieux are both Doctors of the Church, and Edith Stein (Teresa Benedicta of the Cross) is a patron saint of Europe. All were Carmelites, and thus they can be associated with the contemplative mission of St. John. St. Faustina Kowalska, a member of the Congregation of the Sisters of Our Lady of Mercy, is one of the biggest names in contemporary spirituality. She is the most recent in a long line of female mystics who have encouraged devotion to the Sacred Heart and trust in Christ's mercy. Earlier names in this lineage include St. Margaret Mary Alacoque, St. Gertrude the Great, and St. Mechtilde. In the past century, women have also played a significant role in the foundation of new ecclesial movements. In addition to Speyr, Chiara Lubich and Carmen Hernández are the most noteworthy examples here.

Two of my favorite exemplars of the feminine genius are St. Jadwiga, queen of Poland (1373–1399), the patroness of the great Jagiellonian University in Kraków, and Ida Friederike Görres (1901–1971), a writer who found consolation in the theological works of Joseph Ratzinger before he was famous. In the midst of the theological chaos of the 1960s, Görres described Ratzinger in letters to a friend as her "prophet in Israel"—the one voice she found to be a credible interpreter of the documents of the Second Vatican Council—and the potential "theological conscience of the German Church," no less. Görres also wrote significant works on the lives of the saints.

Whoever may be the reader's own heroines and exemplars of the feminine genius, I warmly commend this collection of essays by faithful Catholic women striving to put this gift of their creation at the service of the Church.

Professor Tracey Rowland
University of Notre Dame (Australia)

Acknowledgments

Rachel Bulman

This book would not be possible without the vision of Word on Fire and especially the Publishing team. While there are many books exploring femininity, I believe this book, with its pointed focus and expert writers, stands out among the rest.

Thank you to the women who took the time to contribute to this project and continually invite all people into the intellectual life through their vocations, work, and ministry.

Thank you to the women who have paved the way for the feminine mind, many of whom are mentioned in this book, and to those who work tirelessly today in study and thought.

Through the intercession of Mary, Our Blessed Mother, Seat of Wisdom, may this book open the mind to the possibility and fruition of the genius of women.

Introduction

Rachel Bulman

I was almost ten years old when Disney released its animated *Beauty and the Beast*. An avid reader, I saw myself in Belle, simultaneously mortified and proud at the way her intellect was prodded throughout the movie:

> Look, there she goes, that girl is so peculiar
> I wonder if she's feeling well
> With a dreamy, far-off look
> And her nose stuck in a book
> What a puzzle to the rest of us is Belle.

Belle presented a different way of living to a town lost in the monotony of everyday life ("every morning just the same"). Her love of reading and her different way of thinking were so abnormal to the townspeople that many thought she might even be ill!

At the close of that opening song, we meet Gaston: the self-absorbed, muscular, obnoxiously "masculine" antagonist. He snatches her book: "How can you read this? There's no pictures!" Certainly a harmless observation, but eventually he dabbles in the ridiculous: "It's not right for a woman to read. Soon she starts getting ideas . . . and thinking!"

Belle was disarming, not only because of her beauty, but because of her desire to seek something outside of herself. She couldn't travel and the internet didn't exist, so she sought to know the world outside of her village through the pages of books. She exercised her intellect in such a way that it impacted her entire world. There was a wistfulness and a wisdom about her manifested by the expansion of her mind.

In Luke 2, after the birth of Christ, the shepherds make known what they had been told about Jesus, and Mary "treasured all these words and pondered them in her heart" (Luke 2:19). This passage is often used to support the contemplative and quiet life of the Blessed Mother, but I'd like to draw our attention to two other elements within this verse: the heart and reflection.

Women are entirely geared toward receptivity, and this disposition creates a unique affective life. I consider my emotional life to be a superpower, and like all superpowers, it must be bridled, controlled, and tempered. For affectivity to bear fruit, it must be purified with the intellect and the will.

Our Lady's heart is a place of solace and safety. There is no temptation to waywardness or extreme irrationality. Her will was so united to the will of God that her reflection, her ability to utilize her intellect and her mind to understand what was before her, continued to predispose her heart, her affectivity, her emotion toward the will of the Father. Our Lady invites us to purify our affective life through active intellectual engagement.

St. Edith Stein explains, "Intellect and emotion must cooperate in a particular way in order to transmute the purely emotional attitudes into one cognizant of values."[1] Both intellect and emotion are necessary for a full life. They work simultaneously to actualize the human person, avoiding extremes that are commonplace when the intellect or emotion operate alone without the balance of the other.

The heart of the woman is valuable, and the mind of the woman is valuable too.

"Feminine genius" has become a bit of a buzzword, but the fullness of all femininity has yet to be exhausted. There have been many great female thinkers.

---

1. Edith Stein, *Essays on Women*, trans. Freda Mary Oben (Washington, DC: ICS Publications 1996), 104.

While entering into the intellectual life is a special call for some women, each woman must tap into her ability to become a lover of wisdom because of *the woman* par excellence: the Blessed Virgin Mary. She is the embodiment of femininity for us. She not only pursues wisdom but loves Wisdom himself; in fact, the early Church Fathers called her the "Seat of Wisdom." If you seek to become more like our Lady, then you are also seeking to become a thinker. Within her flesh, Mary allowed the divine to come among us. She made the unreachable reachable and brought that which seemed far within the grasp of mankind. As thinkers, as women, we seek to do that too.

In *Fides et Ratio*, John Paul the Great teaches us that Mary's fiat does not impair her humanity or freedom, but rather expands her very person.[2] Her love of wisdom expands who she is. Your desire to be a thinker, to answer the greatest "whys" that arise in your own heart and in the hearts of those around you, not only brings light to the Gospel truth but also allows it to rise to its highest fulfillment.

In 1946, *The Intellectual Life* by A.G. Sertillanges, OP, was published. The first time I read this book, I devoured it. It was a brilliant concoction of abstract and pragmatic advice for anyone desiring to read, write, study, and be holy. But when this book is read against the backdrop of the world today, it is obvious that a female approach to this topic is needed. While I wouldn't dare to position this group of essays as a feminine replacement for Sertillanges' brilliance, I do hope this book will provide the beginning of a much-needed conversation—and even beg you, the reader, to ask questions of yourself. Each essay intends to call us into femininity with a special emphasis on the rational, creative, powerful, and beautiful mind of the woman.

Fulton Sheen once said, "To a great extent the level of any civilization is the level of its womanhood."[3] While this book invites all women to cultivate the life of the mind, I have a special hope these pages are read by young mothers, young career women, college students, and even high school students. May these younger minds have the courage to challenge our

---

2. John Paul II, *Fides et Ratio*, 108, encyclical letter, September 14, 1998, vatican.va.
3. Fulton J. Sheen, *Life Is Worth Living* (New York: McGraw-Hill, 1953), 75.

civilization to grow in knowledge and virtue and maybe even use this book as a guide in doing so.

Apropos of the theme, the intellectual life is not always what one may think it to be. I know that one of my greatest obstacles to enriching my mind is the lie that, in order to think, I must devote myself to hours of reading and some sort of academic work. While these are good things and things that I practice when I have the chance, they are not the formula to sparking the fire of the mind.

I believe that the Lord, in his wisdom, has surrounded you with current opportunities to think deeply. You can fan the flame of thought in the mountains on a hike, in a library buried in a stack of books, while you nurse your infant child, watching the storylines of your favorite sitcom unfold, or while doing the thing you do each day that you call "work." We must realize that the pursuit of God is not confined to any framework precisely because he pursues you tirelessly in every single moment of your life.

What does pursuing the intellectual life look like for you? I think there are as many ways to answer this question as there are women in the world. But it will begin with the things that you love. It will set those things afire, and the flames will spread throughout your entire life.

For me, it began with Theology of the Body and expanded outward. It now envelopes how I write, how I teach, how I mother, how I think, and how I love. There is a fullness herein that I never imagined possible. But when I neglect any aspect of self—mind, heart, or body—the fullness is lessened.

When I grow weary of writing or reading or thinking or searching, I crawl underneath the mantle of Our Lady. She covers me in her cloak and whispers away the distractions that say that I am not a thinker, that this is too hard, that this is all for naught. And she whispers them away with one word: "Fiat." Yes to this. Yes to his will. Yes to becoming woman fully alive and in pursuit.

The monks in Christian antiquity called Our Lady "the table at which faith sits in thought." Beloved daughter, pull up a chair. Rest beneath this cloak and hear it even now. Yes, the intellectual life is for you. Let's sit together and think.

Foundations of the Intellectual Life

Sr. Josephine Garrett

In a world without brokenness, woundedness, and confusion, this essay would be a simple sentence. In a world where we were naturally able to order ourselves and our lives toward the one thing, the highest good, so many words would not be needed. Yet, we are broken and striving, and so we need long essays and long roads. In a perfect world, we would simply say, the prerequisite to the intellectual life is love. St. Paul writes, "If I speak in the tongues of mortals and of angels, but do not have love, I am a noisy gong or a clanging cymbal. And if I have prophetic powers, and understand all mysteries and all knowledge, and if I have all faith, so as to remove mountains, but do not have love, I am nothing" (1 Cor. 13:1–2). I heard it said once that all knowledge, whether it is wise enough to be religiously affiliated or not, is a grace. All expression of truth, whether overtly religious or not, is an expression of God's love and desire to reveal himself to us. Love of God is the prerequisite to the intellectual life, and this love ought to move beyond prerequisite and permeate and sustain the intellectual life; without it, the world will have received yet another resounding gong. Love is simply to will the good of the other. So, how do we love God? By wanting what God wants, by willing with our will what God wills. But, in order to know how to make this response of love, we need to know how to have a conversation with the Beloved. The prerequisite of love of God is cultivated in silence and lived out in prayer, and its fruit is a desire to learn that is ordered toward the Beloved.

1

Silence

Our lives have become full of patterns and tendencies that mute silence. I became aware of this when I was first exposed to intentional silence. I noticed that my spiritual directors considered titration the best practice when forming someone in silence. I was told that an eight-day silent retreat was not advisable if I had not completed a three-day silent retreat, and that a thirty-day silent retreat was not advisable if I had not completed several eight-day silent retreats. This advice communicated to me that most of us do not have a natural tolerance for silence, and we must build this tolerance up over time. It was interesting to me and seemed a little silly, but once I sought intentional silence, I understood. Silence is loud and can be a threat to the self-serving egos we slowly and subtly build up over time. It is full of a sound that we simply don't abide with often; it is full of a sound that egocentrism must bow down to. Simply put, silence is full of God's voice.

In his book on silence, Cardinal Sarah makes bold claims regarding silence. He says not only that God's voice is silence but that God is silence.[1] To seek the intellectual life without being at home with silence means I seek a gift from God apart from God. I want the things of God without God himself, because all knowledge is a grace and a free gift from God. To seek the intellectual life without a growing discipline of being at home with silence indicates that I have made God an object for my use instead of the object of my love.

Throughout Scripture, we see God calling and encountering man to and in places of emptiness, places of silence, to speak to the heart and express the nature of his love. "Therefore, I will now allure her, and bring her into the wilderness" (Hosea 2:14), "I remember the devotion of your youth, your love as a bride, how you followed me in the wilderness" (Jer. 2:2), "He sustained him in a desert land, in a howling wilderness waste; he shielded him, cared for him, guarded him as the apple of his eye" (Deut. 32:10). The emptiness of

---

1. Robert Cardinal Sarah, *The Power of Silence: Against the Dictatorship of Noise* (San Francisco: Ignatius Press, 2017), 22.

silence is pregnant with advent promises. To properly receive the fruits and gifts of the intellectual life, silence disposes us to wait, ready to receive the Lord himself in our intellectual pursuits.

I remember when I was preparing to leave for my own thirty-day silent retreat, I was having a conversation with my provincial superior and it came up that I was taking some ministry work with me on the trip to finish on the first day I would be at the retreat center. She gently corrected me, saying, "Sister Josephine, I would like you to depart for your retreat empty-handed; please do not take any work on the trip with you, and arrive there ready to receive what God has for you." Today, the place of silence we are each called to is not somewhere out there. Cardinal Sarah also notes that inside each person there is an inner silence.[2] The wilderness and desert we are called to is in ourselves. The seed of the Word is there, ready to be formed, ready to take root in our intellectual lives, among other things, and bear fruit for the Kingdom.

This notion of prerequisites should not be misunderstood. We do not pass the silence course and check the silence box. A more appropriate term might be predispositions, dispositions that we foster and carry with us into the intellectual life as safeguards from the tendencies of concupiscence, the tendencies of our insecurities, and the tendencies of our fears. Our entire life will be a coming home to silence, to where, in the end, there will be no words, only the Word.[3]

Prayer

It seems so obvious, it seems too obvious, but I will not cease to proclaim the primacy of prayer, because with each passing day I believe more and more that we are in the midst of a crisis of prayer in our Church. I asked a friend once, based on his experience as a pastor, how much time he thought most people sincerely spent in private prayer and meditation per day. His response was perhaps two to five minutes at best. Approaching the intellectual life

---

2. Sarah, 22.
3. See *Catechism of the Catholic Church* 65.

without proximity to the Father through prayer is like drawing water from a well with a teaspoon instead of a bucket. Significant human effort will be put forth with very little gain.

The fruit of a prayerless disposition in the intellectual life will likely be conviction after conviction from the Holy Spirit while standing amazed before others who appear to put forth less effort, who have fewer degrees and are far less well read, yet are soaring to intellectual heights that remain inaccessible to the one who lacks prayer. This is the justice and mercy of God. "He has shown strength with his arm; he has scattered the proud in the thoughts of their hearts. He has brought down the powerful from their thrones, and lifted up the lowly; he has filled the hungry with good things, and sent the rich away empty" (Luke 1:51–53).

If we were asked to choose between prayer or breathing, I would hope the choice would be prayer. Not because I advocate for not valuing the life-giving effects of breath, but because we must understand that without an ongoing relationship with the Father, we would not have been able to draw the last breath we just drew. The relationship that God is in with each of us is so detailed that God attends to each breath we take. Each breath is included and considered in his providence. Before this kind of relationship, all prayer is seen as a drop in the bucket by way of a response to God. Yet, God is generous and all loving. Those drops are pleasing before him, accompanied by and rising to him with the help of the Holy Spirit, and they soothe the thirst of the heart of Jesus. It is an opportunity for prayer in and of itself to contemplate the depth of the longing that God has for us that allows our response of drops to the overflowing stream of his love to somehow be satisfying to him. Because God is generous, he will permit us to the intellectual life even if we have neglected prayer. But because he is merciful, if we persist in a lack of prayer we will inevitably face frustrations and difficulties; this is loving chastisement from the Father, an invitation in the form of difficulties to allow us to turn toward him.

What might your daily prayer look like? It can be quite simple. I encourage you to remain with Scripture, perhaps one of the readings of the day. Spiritual books are wonderful, but for our conversations with God, his Word is a best practice beginning point. Using the tradition of *lectio divina* for at least fifteen minutes of prayer can suffice for beginners. I also highly encourage keeping a prayer journal so you can jot down a couple of things that come to you during those fifteen minutes. This will allow you to look back over time and discover themes in your conversation with God, much like you would with a friend. I would also encourage praying with the Liturgy of the Hours, the prayer of the Church; but keep the practice of noting what stands out to you. The key is tuning in to God's voice. With a life of prayer, cultivated in silence, our pursuits in the intellectual life will blossom before us: "Instead of the thorn shall come up the cypress; instead of the brier shall come up the myrtle; and it shall be to the Lord for a memorial, for an everlasting sign that shall not be cut off" (Isa. 55:13).

Desire to Learn

At the end of the day, once we have cultivated silence and a life of prayer, the desire for the intellectual life will overflow, in right order, and be centered on plumbing "the depths of God" or "the perfection of the Almighty" (Job 11:7 NABRE). In this case, go for it! Do not tire of exploring aspects of our faith; read the *Catechism of the Catholic Church* and participate in Bible studies to enhance your knowledge of Scripture and increase your comfort with encountering the Word in the Word. Read the lives of the saints! Read and study the writings of our Church Fathers. Read for yourself Vatican II documents. Do not let news outlets and media outlets do your thinking for you. Root the fulfilment of intellectual life as often as you can in primary resources. Through the cultivation of silence and prayer, you will now be learning through him, with him, and in him. Right order is key. If desire to learn precedes the cultivation of silence and the life of prayer, we run the risk of making idols of our intellectual lives. Do not hop around the golden calf idol for the likes of men. You will be exhausted, frustrated, and spiritually barren, without fruit. Fix the gaze of your desires on the Beloved, as he has fixed his gaze on you, the apple of his eye. The Hebrew translation of this phrase, "the apple of God's eye," is more properly translated as "the little man in God's eye." In your intellectual life, fix your gaze back on the Father, who reflects you in his eye. Seek to know him as he knows you—to the depths. Soar to the heights of love by surrendering the gift of your intellect, given to you by the Father, back to the Father. This will take your whole life, and rightly so; and one day you will see him face to face and know him. And thanks, in part, to the gift of your intellectual life, you will be at home with this eternal love.

The Virtues and the Intellectual Life

Susanna Spencer

Imagine you are sitting down to do some serious reading. All is quiet, and you are alone. You reach to pick up your book, but, hesitating, decide to do a quick email check. You open an email from your favorite news source. Reading news is important, you think to yourself. But the book nags at your conscience. You lock your phone, but instead of reading decide to make a cup of tea. A nice hot cup of tea will help you rest in the intellectual effort you are about to undertake. The tea is finally brewing, and you go back to your desk.

Glancing at the clock, you realize you have used up ten of your thirty minutes. Discouragement hits you, and you rack your brain to plan time for additional reading. Five minutes later you are finally opening your book. You read a few lines, and your phone pings. You pick it up and tap out a quick reply. You wonder if it is worth reading with only ten minutes left. But you decide it is—you really do want to have a more intellectual life. Yet your bad habits are making it hard to commit to work. You need to learn to overcome these bad habits and grow in virtue.

The intellectual life is so much more than engaging ourselves intellectually. One must also form oneself in a life of virtue. Along with all the other virtues, we need prudence to determine what and when we will study, temperance for self-discipline, studiousness to focus on important knowledge, and an internal recollection to help us focus on the truths worth pursuing. These are all moral virtues, rational habits, which we either form by intentionally doing a good act until the act has become easy to choose or receive as infused virtues from the Lord. They are not mechanical habits that one does not think about doing, such as flipping on the light switch or buckling a seatbelt. A rational habit is rational and intentional, because even when it is ingrained in one's subconscious, one must choose with one's will to do the act. Further, a mechanical habit may falsely appear as a rational habit when an intentional choice is not involved. For example, we might habitually thank someone for helping us, but it lacks the virtue of gratitude without an intentional act of thankfulness united with our feelings.

The Catholic tradition has classified virtues into natural virtues and infused virtues. A natural virtue is one that we can form without the help of grace; these are the virtues that the ancient, pre-Christian philosophers such as Aristotle defined and promoted in their writings, explaining that virtue is necessary for human happiness. Examples of these are gratitude, friendliness, and studiousness. Each of the natural virtues are part of the cardinal virtues of prudence, fortitude, justice, and temperance. With prudence we take right knowledge and apply it practically, such as when doing research before making a purchase. With fortitude we persevere in doing some good, such as when patiently helping a child sound out a word. With justice we give to others what is due to them. And with temperance we moderate our desires. To form a virtue naturally, we must intentionally choose to do acts that are like that virtue again and again until we are able to choose them without interior resistance and it has become a rational habit. When we struggle to form a virtue naturally, the Lord can help us by offering us infused virtues. Infused virtues must be consciously chosen and participated in with the help of grace. God can infuse in us the natural virtues, but he also offers us the theological virtues—which we cannot have naturally—of faith, hope, and charity. Infused virtues are a great gift for growing in holiness and the intellectual life, for the Lord can help us perform good acts even when we are not perfect. For example, we can ask him to help us grow in studiousness with the help of his grace, and the more we cooperate with his grace, the more we are inclined to both cooperate with his grace in other areas and grow in studiousness.

To have any of the virtues fully, we must have all of the virtues. They are all connected to each other and cannot be fully understood separate from each other. As St. Gregory the Great explains, "One virtue without the other is either of no account whatever, or very imperfect."[1]

Since all the virtues are connected, if we are called to any of the virtues, which we are, we are called to have all the virtues. This means that there are not specifically masculine or feminine virtues. What makes a virtue distinctive for a woman is that she has those virtues as a woman: she is courageous as a woman, she is patient as a woman, she is prudent as a woman, and she is studious as a woman. Further, her virtues are distinctive because they are her virtues and no one else's. When I have a virtue, I have it as myself and as a woman. My virtues have a specific "Susanna-ness" that looks different in me than in any other person because I am a unique individual. Philosopher Dietrich von Hildebrand talks about individuality as "the particular, unique, and inimitable thought in the mind of God which every human being embodies." Our individuality is at its best when we become virtuous and strip away all that makes us less like God. Hildebrand explains:

> It is only in a saint that individuality thus conceived can fully display itself. For it contains, on the one hand, the particular natural character of the person which, however, never implies defects and imperfections as such; and on the other hand, a supernatural transfiguration and elevation of that particular nature.[2]

As women in pursuit of the intellectual life, then, we are called to have all the virtues and to focus especially on prudence, temperance, studiousness, and recollection. As we pursue them, we must pursue them as ourselves in our

---

1. Quoted in Thomas Aquinas, *Summa theologiae* 1-2.65.1.
2. Dietrich von Hildebrand, *Transformation in Christ* (Manchester, NH: Sophia Institute Press, 1990), 20.

own particular vocations. When we do this, we become more virtuous, more ourselves, and more like Christ. Let us look more specifically at what virtues we especially need to pursue an intellectual life.

Prudence and Temperance

The clock ticks by. The two hours I have for writing are almost used up. I realize that if I am going to hit my deadline, I must write more today. I think through what I have left to do that day: cook dinner, eat dinner with the family, ensure the kids clean the kitchen, family prayer time, story time, and then the short sweet two hours in the evening before my husband and I go to bed. Maybe I can write more while the kids clean the kitchen, and then again for an hour after they go to bed. My husband and I always make a point to spend at least part of our evening together.

I would not have been able to make this plan without the virtue of prudence, the virtue that helps you know the right way to apply the right knowledge you have. It resides in what St. Thomas Aquinas calls our "practical reason"[3] and is the practical application of truth. It is an important virtue for every person, not just those in pursuit of the intellectual life. Prudence is an essential part of laying the foundation for growing in an intellectual life.

Often the pursuit of the intellectual life will have to be done in snatches. While we may plan two hours on one day, more likely than not it will be snatches of time here and there—snatches that we discover with the virtue of prudence. We might take our current read to the quiet of the bathroom instead of our phone. We might put on that stimulating podcast or deep audiobook instead of going for something lightweight and easy. We might use a quiet moment to consider a concept we have been reading about or simply place ourselves closer to God rather than let our minds wander. Prudence does not negate a plan but allows for the plan to be executed according to one's reality.

---

3. Thomas Aquinas, *ST* 2-2.47.2.

In addition to the cardinal virtue of prudence, one seeking to live the intellectual life needs the virtue of temperance. We have temperance when we have the self-control to always do and desire the right thing. Temperance is not merely being able to resist sinful inclinations; one who is completely temperate is free from even immoderate inclinations. While we will not likely become fully temperate, we can take steps in that direction by mortifying various desires through penances, such as fasting or blocking distracting websites. Doing this will help us overcome our irrational desires and direct our good desires to what is truly best for us to do.

How do we grow in the virtues of prudence and temperance? For me, growing in prudence in time management has often meant seeking counsel from my husband as to how to make time for me to work. He thoroughly supports my endeavors and helps me balance them with my duties toward our children and our household. He also splits with me many of the household duties that are traditionally held to be in the domain of the woman so that I can have more time to invest in my intellectual life.

Regular confession and spiritual direction are first steps to growing in temperance, especially if you are like me and confess sins of intemperance at every confession. My spiritual director also helps me work to implement resolutions to help me become more temperate. Two ways to check on your resolutions are to have an accountability partner and to make multiple "examens" throughout the day. An examen takes only a few minutes. First, you go to a quiet space mentally and physically (as circumstances allow). Then you meditate over each moment since your last examen, asking yourself if each act brought you closer to God or further from God. When you find that it brought you closer, you thank God for the grace you received to do good things. In reflecting upon acts where you turned away from God, you repent over where you failed to respond to grace. You finish by making a firm resolution to do better the rest of the day, making a practical plan to follow the resolution, and asking God for the grace to do better.

Studiousness

My lunch digesting, I slipped into the quiet of the Mac Lab on my college campus and glanced at the clock. I had four quiet hours at my student work desk, where only a few students would need help on those long summer afternoons. Graduate theology summer sessions were intense at my university—just three short weeks to learn the content of a class and do all the classwork. Thankfully, my summer job made it easy to get work done. Yet, unfortunately for my intellectual temperance, Facebook was in its infancy, only navigable by college students. Every weekday that summer, I had four long hours, three hundred pages to read, and all the internet at my fingertips. One would think that I would have overcome the temptation to distraction and curiosity years ago, but when paired with my weakness to give into sloth, I never have been as studious as I ought to be. And I have wasted more hours than I would like to admit.

Studiousness is one of the essential virtues for pursuing the intellectual life. Simply defined, it is care for important knowledge and is "about the desire and study in the pursuit of knowledge."[4] It is the virtue that helps us care to know the right things and stay focused on those right things. There are many ways we can fail to be studious, such as through curiosity or sloth. The vice of curiosity is not just a desire to know things but to seek to know things that are not important to know or not good to know, or to know things at the wrong time and in the wrong way. For example, it may be good to be informed about world events, but when one is called to the intellectual life, it is better and more virtuous to put the pursuit of higher knowledge first. We need studiousness and temperance to help focus on this good.

Another vice that makes it harder to be studious is that of sloth or acedia. While some may think of sloth as merely being lazy, this is not the case. Sloth is deeper and more insidious than mere laziness. It is having sorrow over the good in your life.[5] It is being surrounded by blessings—such as a good job,

---

4. Thomas Aquinas, *ST* 2-2.167.2.
5. Thomas Aquinas, *ST* 2-2.35.4.

a comfortable home, healthy food, a family, God's free gift of grace—and desiring something other than these good things. It is what makes you feel oppressed by your life and duties and wish you could do anything but that. It is the temptation that plants the idea to waste your time and leads you to create the habit of doomscrolling when you should be reading a book or writing an essay. But it is not just limited to work time. It leads you to hide in your bathroom with your phone watching videos online and to check for notifications while sharing a meal with others. It is poison to any joy the Lord is offering you in your everyday, repetitive life.

If we want to grow in the virtue of studiousness we need to work to root out curiosity and sloth in all parts of our lives. This means we must look at each of our activities and ask ourselves if they are helping us grow in virtue. St. Paul tells us, "Whatever is true, whatever is honorable, whatever is just, whatever is pure, whatever is pleasing, whatever is commendable, if there is any excellence and if there is anything worthy of praise, think about these things. Keep on doing the things that you have learned and received and heard and seen in me, and the God of peace will be with you" (Phil. 4:8–9).

We should look at all we allow to enter our minds through articles, websites, books, movies, shows, and music and ask if it is helping to form us to be more studious or to be more susceptible to temptations of curiosity and sloth.

We need to take these things seriously to prayer, especially with the words of the mystic Julian of Norwich. She wrote about the Lord's great love for us and his desire for us to know him. In our pursuit of truth we are pursuing him; our desire for knowledge is good and is meant to lead us to the Lord. For "we can never stop wishing or longing until we fully and joyfully possess him, and then we shall wish for nothing more; for he wants us to be absorbed in knowing and loving him until the time when we reach fulfillment in heaven."[6] This leads us to understanding another virtue central to having a fruitful intellectual life.

---

6. Julian of Norwich, *Revelations of Divine Love*, trans. Elizabeth Spearing (London: Penguin Books, 1998), 50.

Recollection

To truly grow in forming our minds, we must grow in the virtue of recollection. When we are recollected we are able to set "ourselves at a distance from all present concerns" and order "all things before the face of God,"[7] seeing all things with a view to our ultimate union with him. While we can foster it within ourselves, recollection can only be received as a gift from God as we dispose our souls to be more open to him.

When we are recollected, we have learned to place ourselves continually in the presence of God. To do this takes a repetition of countless intentional acts of calling God's presence to our minds. It means taking daily time for quiet prayer, going to regular Adoration, and learning to meet God in the quiet of our souls no matter what is going on around us. God has dwelt within our souls from the moment of our Baptisms, and it is here that we must pursue him continually, setting aside anything that keeps us from him. St. Teresa of Avila wrote to her sisters:

> You know that God is everywhere. . . . Recall that Saint Augustine tells us about his seeking God in many places and eventually finding him within himself. A soul that is often distracted needs to understand this truth in order to speak to its Eternal Father and to take its delight in him.[8]

We must pursue God within our souls continually. As St. Teresa says:

> Those who are able to shut themselves up in this little heaven of the soul, wherein the Maker of heaven and earth dwells, and who have formed the habits of looking at nothing and staying in no place that distracts the senses, may be sure that they are walking on an excellent road.[9]

---

7. Hildebrand, *Transformation*, 111.
8. Teresa of Avila, *The Way of Perfection*, trans. Henry Carrigan Jr. (Brewster, MA: Paraclete Press, 2009), 114.
9. Teresa of Avila, 115.

To do this we must seek to overcome curiosity and distraction, which Hildebrand describes as the "exact antithesis to recollection" and "a state of being dragged along from one object to another, never touching any of them but superficially."[10] Hildebrand explains that growing in recollection also means giving up some things we enjoy—it means limiting the time we spend becoming drained by "empty and superficial conversations" and "shun[ning] everything that appeals to our craving for sensation."[11] It goes along with what St. Paul wrote to the Philippians—we habituate ourselves to dwell on only what is good and pure.

As we pursue the virtues necessary for the intellectual life, recollection will remind us that the point of this pursuit is to gain knowledge of the truth. The pursuit of truth leads us to the love of God. When we know truth, we know God, and when we know who God truly is, we cannot help but love him and have happiness.

As we seek to grow in these virtues, we must remember that they are not the end, but that God is: "For recollection proper always means an awakening to the essential, a recourse to the absolute which never ceases to be all-important and in whose light alone everything else discloses its true meaning."[12]

---

10. Hildebrand, *Transformation*, 105.
11. Hildebrand, 106.
12. Hildebrand, 106.

Healing and Knowing the Truth

Sr. Miriam James Heidland

And you will know the truth, and the truth will make you free.
—JOHN 8:32

Have you ever had the piercing experience of knowing something was true in your mind and yet feeling the stinging pain in your heart of a reality that seems to contradict that truth?

Have you ever felt deep anger or self-contempt over a distressing experience in your life and said to yourself or to another person, "I know theoretically that God has not forgotten me and that he loves me, but I feel so abandoned, alone, and ashamed in this place. My heart hurts so deeply and I don't know what to do." When this happens, we often chide ourselves for not having enough faith in God, or we make agreements with lies that maybe God really does not love us or that we are an exception to his forgiveness and mercy.

We can know something intellectually but have a seemingly different lived reality. At that point, we usually eschew one side of the equation. We grasp on to what we know intellectually and push away the different experiences of our hearts, or we tend to our hearts and either sentimentalize God or relate to him from a narrow and distorted view. While we all have gradations of these tendencies within each of us, I would like to propose that healing (becoming whole and in communion with God) ourselves and others is not an either/or reality but by necessity a both/and reality.

We can know through revelation that God is love, digest that truth in CCD and theology classes, and write dissertations on Trinitarian love and the sovereignty of God, and yet still be crushed by the weight of rejection, abandonment, isolation, and abuse and behave in our daily lives largely out of these broken and agonizing paradigms.

We must know intellectually the truth about God and allow this knowledge to continually be grown, purified, and refined, and we must also "know" on a deep and intimate level the truth about God in the depths of our hearts, in our inner room, our lived experiences, especially in moments of both deep desire and deep suffering.

In his book *Jesus of Nazareth: From the Baptism in the Jordan to the Transfiguration*, Pope Benedict XVI writes, "Healing is an essential dimension of the apostolic mission and of Christianity. When understood at a sufficiently deep level, this expresses the entire content of redemption."[1] The healing that God brings is not superficial or shallow. As we study salvation history, we see that healing and deliverance is always ordered toward communion and relationship. God is always liberating his creation from sin, from the enemy, from fragmentation and bringing his creation back into communion and wholeness. This is what the truth of God, who is love, does. Love unites, heals, purifies, and brings into communion and wholeness.

This reality is foundational in our personal lives and our interior worlds in a particular way. All of us have places within our hearts, minds, bodies, and souls that are in bondage and are fragmented. All of us have places where our hearts are hard, where we serve other gods, where we fear to trust or be dependent and vulnerable. In these places we become self-reliant, trying to "fix" the painful places ourselves or grasp onto another person or an elusive salve for our fearful and aching hearts in the hopes that the pain will stop and that love will be restored. In the grasping and self-reliance, we "miss the mark" and place ourselves, others, and things in the place of God, who alone is the divine physician of whom we all have need.

---

1. Pope Benedict XVI, *Jesus of Nazareth: From the Baptism in the Jordan to the Transfiguration* (New York: Doubleday, 2007), 176.

Knowing the truth, both intellectually and experientially, is what sets us free. It is knowing about Jesus and who he reveals himself to be as well as knowing him personally and knowing who he reveals himself to be in every experience of our lives. We must know both ways so we can live in the freedom of the children of God. Jesus comes to reconcile all things to the Father, and this includes every single part of our hearts, minds, bodies, and souls.

How does this work? Let us apply it to our personal experience. What is something that has been troubling you lately? Perhaps it's an ongoing disagreement with your spouse in which you feel undesirable and unloved. Perhaps it's the presence of a co-worker who triggers fear and anxiety in your heart and always seems to have the last say in all your interactions. Perhaps it is an addiction, general anxiety about the future or current events, or a relationship with a parent or friend that is not as close as you wish it to be. Ask the Holy Spirit to reveal to you an area of your life to focus upon.

Notice what comes to the surface of your heart as that situation/person comes into view in your mind's eye. What are the honest thoughts that arise when you think of it/them? Be very attentive to the emotions that arise with the thoughts as well. Our emotions are clues to what we truly believe about something/someone. Ask the Holy Spirit to reveal to you what you are believing about yourself in that situation. Be very honest. The beliefs often sound like this: "I am all alone, I cannot trust anyone, I have to fix this all by myself, I am dirty, I am ugly, no one gets me, I can't tell anyone, it's my fault, I will never have the love that I truly desire," etc. The beliefs that are etched into our daily experiences are very powerful and dictate how we live our lives.

As you notice these things in your heart, I would like to invite you to very vulnerably ask Jesus to show you the truth of who you are in this situation and how he loves you in this very place. Ask Jesus to reveal the truth of who he is and who you are in this moment of suffering. You do not have to strive or tell yourself nice things; allow Jesus to speak to you.

As you experience Jesus in this place, test the revelation in your heart against the truth of who Jesus reveals himself to be in Scripture and Tradition. God does not contradict himself. Even when the Lord speaks a challenging truth to us, he always does so in love with the impetus toward repair, reconciliation, and communion. Repeat the truth of what Jesus says within your heart. Let the eternal truth echo within you and forge new pathways in your heart and mind. Each time we do this, we are transformed on a deeper level.

This very experience is exactly what is happening to the woman caught in adultery in John 8:1–11. We see a woman brought into the middle of a condemning public spectacle because people in her life wanted to exploit her sinfulness. Yet Jesus attends to every aspect of this situation in a very particular way. Jesus evokes the truth in both the men who wanted to stone her (who were just using her to trap Jesus) and within the woman herself. As she stands before the men, exposed and humiliated, Jesus appeals to what she is believing about herself and the truth of who he is and who she is.

After inviting the men to consider their own interior state and corresponding exterior actions, Jesus bends down to the ground to write in the dirt. In the truth of their inability to rightfully condemn her, the men depart, leaving Jesus alone with the woman. From the ground, the King of heaven looks up at her. In profound kindness and strength he says to her, "Woman, where are they? Has no one condemned you?"

"No one, sir," she quietly replies.

And then he speaks the truth to her hurting heart, mind, body, and soul in deep love and freedom as he declares, "Neither do I condemn you. Go your way, and from now on do not sin again" (John 8:11).

I can imagine that these words were like water to her parched life on every level. His words and his love challenged everything she was believing about herself and her actions therein. I can also imagine that she thought about Jesus and the words he spoke to her and the love he showed her over and over again, every time washing her heart anew in freedom and mercy. In one of her most shameful experiences, love literally intervened and interrupted her sin, self-contempt, and sorrow. This is Jesus. This is healing. This is the truth.

It would have done the woman no good to deny the truth of her sin or her feelings or how humiliated she felt. Only in honesty are we healed and brought into wholeness. Only in the truth is there freedom. She received Jesus that day in truth, and that truth and love set her free. She knew him. And so must we. This knowing is a lifelong process that expands and grows little by little, day by day. Because love never ends, healing is always occurring.

Isaiah 53:4–5 majestically proclaims, "Surely he has borne our infirmities and carried our diseases; yet we accounted him stricken, struck down by God, and afflicted. But he was wounded for our transgressions, crushed for our iniquities; upon him was the punishment that made us whole, and by his bruises we are healed."

God is with us. He never leaves us nor forsakes us. He goes before us. Jesus has suffered everything we have ever suffered in love and in truth, and in him is our home. There is not a moment of our lives that is outside the sovereignty of God or where he is not present. He is always there and desires to heal all things and bring us home to his heart.

We can have experiences of being abandoned and rejected by people and still know and experience in the core of our being that we are neither rejected nor abandoned in our identity. We can suffer trauma and helplessness and powerlessness and know that this is not our identity nor the end of the story of our lives. Jesus teaches us that it is through, with, and in him that our lives are ushered into passion, death, and resurrection. This is the promise of our Baptism, that we belong to God and he to us.

This life with Jesus is not just intellectually knowing something or knowing objective truth but the reception of that truth into the emotional and experiential realm of our hearts and lives. It is receiving the truth into ourselves, into the experiences of isolation, fragmentation, and sorrow and of hope, beauty, and joy. It is receiving Jesus in every way and allowing him to receive us in every way. This is transforming union. This is how we are transformed from the darkest places and are brought into his own marvelous light. This is holiness. This is the truth. This is the love that never ends.

Saints and the Intellect

Meg Hunter-Kilmer

There is a temptation in academia to divorce the mind from the soul, as though a scholar mustn't allow her religious beliefs to influence her work. Similarly, many shy away from an intellectual approach to faith not merely because it proves difficult but because it seems dangerous, as though God weren't up for the challenges our questions might pose. But the canon of saints is full of men and women whose faith was fueled by study and whose study was enriched by faith, from St. Perpetua (whose autobiography is the first known document written by a Christian woman) to St. Hildegard of Bingen (a medieval polymath whose work furthered nearly a dozen fields of study) to Bl. Columba Kang Wan-suk (whose cunning protected the only priest in Korea for six years and whose evangelical genius made innumerable converts).

Two twentieth-century women in particular demonstrate the ways in which the intellectual life can nourish the soul by both leading it to faith and drawing it deeper into contemplation. One a German nun, one a Mexican mother; one born to a Jewish family, one baptized when she was two days old. But both St. Edith Stein and Bl. Concepción Cabrera de Armida gave their hearts to the Lord, and both wrote with such powerful wisdom that it seems Christians will be studying their work for generations to come. Through their witness and intercession, may we seek to know God, love him, and serve him with all our heart, soul, strength, and mind.

Edith Stein

Edith Stein (1891–1942) was an intellectual through and through. Her genius was quite clearly a gift from God, as it was her brilliant mind that ultimately brought her to Jesus. Born to a German-Jewish family, Edith was insatiably curious from her earliest childhood. As she wrestled with the opposing philosophies she discovered, she soon came to reject her Jewish faith, making a conscious decision to stop praying when she was a teenager. Still, Edith searched, eventually returning to school for a PhD in philosophy.

While in this program, Edith studied under famed phenomenologist Edmund Husserl (a Jewish convert to Lutheranism) and took classes with Catholic philosopher Max Scheler, whose work was the subject of St. John Paul II's doctoral thesis. Her experience of the genius of these two Christian philosophers impressed upon her the intellectual coherence of the Christian faith. She was not yet a Christian, but neither could she reject Christianity out of hand as a medieval philosophy to be put aside by any thinking person. No, Edith's work as a scholar made Christianity impossible to dismiss without serious consideration. Of her study under Christian phenomenologists, Edith later said, "the barriers of rationalistic prejudices with which I had unwittingly grown up fell, and the world of faith unfolded before me. Persons with whom I associated daily, whom I esteemed and admired, lived in it. At the least, they deserved my giving it some serious reflection."[1]

It was her respect for their intellects that opened the mind of the young philosopher to faith. But before her intellect could really consider the truth of the Catholic faith, Edith's heart had to be moved by the witness of Christians whose lives had been changed because of it. This came to pass through the grief of her friend Anna Reinach, the wife of Edith's teacher Adolf. Both Anna and Adolf had been born Jewish and had converted to Lutheranism. When Adolf was killed in World War I, Edith traveled to be with Anna in her grief. Upon arriving, she was stunned to see the joy that undergirded her

---

1. María Ruiz Scaperlanda, *Edith Stein: The Life and Legacy of St. Teresa Benedicta of the Cross* (Manchester, NH: Sophia Institute Press, 2017), 56.

friend's suffering. Though she suffered deeply in the wake of her husband's death, Anna lived in hope, confident that she would see him again. Edith remarked upon this some years later, saying, "It was my first encounter with the Cross and the divine power that it bestows on those who carry it. For the first time, I was seeing with my very eyes the Church, born from her Redeemer's sufferings, triumphant over the sting of death. That was the moment my unbelief collapsed and Christ shone forth—in the mystery of the Cross."[2]

This attraction to Jesus became a more direct pull toward Catholicism through the witness of a woman in Frankfurt who carried her shopping with her as she stopped to pray at the cathedral. "This was something totally new to me," Edith reflected years later. "In the synagogues and Protestant churches I had visited before, people simply went to services. Here, however, I saw someone coming straight from the busy marketplace into this empty church as if she was going to have an intimate conversation. It was something I never forgot."[3]

But an intellectual like Edith needed a book to draw her fully and finally into the Catholic Church. While on vacation with her friends, she chose a book at random—seemingly at random. But her hand was drawn to the autobiography of St. Teresa of Avila, a Doctor of the Church who was herself the granddaughter of a Jewish convert to Catholicism. In that text, Edith found what she had been looking for in all her years of searching for truth and meaning through philosophy. She read the whole book in one night, then put it down, saying, "This is the truth."[4] Through the work of Teresa of Avila, Edith discovered that (as St. John Paul II put it in his homily for her canonization) "truth had a name: Jesus Christ."[5] The very next day, Edith went out and bought a missal and a catechism. She began attending Mass daily even before her Baptism several months later—a Baptism that devastated her devoutly Jewish mother.

---

2. Scaperlanda, 68.
3. *Teresa Benedicta of the Cross Edith Stein (1891–1942) - Biography*, October 11, 1998, vatican.va.
4. *Teresa Benedicta of the Cross*, vatican.va.
5. Scaperlanda, *Edith Stein*, 49.

After her conversion, Edith's intellectual labor continued with translations of Thomas Aquinas, philosophical lectures, theological essays, an autobiographical attempt to combat antisemitism in Germany, and always many letters. She was an international lecturer, speaking on Catholic womanhood and theology as well as phenomenology. But though she continued to publish book-length works on philosophy, Edith struggled for years to obtain work as a philosophy professor. When the academy was finally ready to admit women to that position, Edith was able to teach for only two semesters before she was made to step down because of her Jewish heritage. Hitler's rise to power had begun, and the antisemitic policies that initially pushed Edith Stein out of the academy and into Carmel would ultimately lead to her death in Auschwitz.

Even as a Carmelite novice, Sr. Teresa Benedicta of the Cross (as she was known in religious life) continued to write and publish. By this point her love of silent prayer meant that writing works of philosophy had begun to feel more like a chore, but she continued (in obedience to her superiors), offering up the frequent interruptions to her work that made it feel like such a penance. For her, the work of the mind was in service to the soul, as her superiors well knew. There was no attempt to quash her intellect, only gratitude for such a mind as hers and encouragement to persevere, however she might have been tempted to leave behind her intellectual work to rest in the God it had brought her to.

Sr. Teresa Benedicta pursued God in mind and heart for the rest of her life until she was famously killed in Auschwitz. But while she was canonized as a martyr, it wasn't her death that made a saint of her but her life, a life of reading, research, and reflection that drew her to the One who is Truth itself. Through painful divisions in her family and through her suffering at the hands of the Nazis, she was sustained because she knew him not merely with her emotions, not merely with her will, not merely with her intellect, but with her whole self.

Bl. Concepción Cabrera de Armida

Unlike Edith Stein, Bl. Concepción Cabrera de Armida (1862–1937) wasn't intellectually insatiable by nature. Conchita (as she was called) attended school only until she was eight or nine years old, when the sisters who ran her school were expelled from Mexico. After that, she had some instruction at home, though most of her free time was spent on piano and voice, at which she excelled. Conchita was being prepared to be a matriarch, not a scholar, so there was little time for an education outside baking, embroidery, cooking, cleaning, and the running of a household. She was given a basic education in the faith and a rather more advanced one in the virtue of generosity, frequently accompanying her mother to visit the sick and attend the dying.

But while Conchita was no adolescent philosopher, she was eager to read as many Christian books as she could get her hands on and from a young age felt called to write. She was drawn to prayer and penance, leading many to expect that the pious young girl would become a religious. Conchita, on the other hand, felt certain she was called to marriage—all the more when, at barely thirteen, she met Pancho Armida at a dance. A month later, Pancho proposed and the two began their nine-year engagement.

Her marriage at twenty-one only strengthened young Conchita's spiritual life. During the first years of her marriage, Conchita felt herself belonging more and more to Jesus, while continuing the business of running a household and raising many small children. When she and Pancho had been married for a decade, Conchita experienced a mystical marriage to Jesus, a phenomenon common enough in the annals of holiness among single or consecrated women but not at all among wives and mothers. For Conchita, as always, this love of Jesus only sent her back to her husband a more loving, generous wife; there was no conflict between her love of God and her love of Pancho. In reflecting on her marriage years later, Conchita wrote, "Never did my love for him, so full of tenderness, hinder me from loving God. I loved him with a great simplicity, as wholly enveloped in my love for Jesus. I did not see there was any other pathway for me to come to God."[6]

Conchita was a woman of deep prayer, a wife and mother who loved to read spiritual texts. But in the midst of her ordinary life, she was encountering God in prayer. Unbeknownst to her family, the unassuming Conchita was a mystic whose experience of God was profoundly intellectual: a series of revelations whose theological complexity leaves their reader in awe. From the age of sixteen, Conchita felt called to write; later she asked for the intercession of St. Teresa of Avila so that she would be able to write well of the Lord. "I always had an inclination to writing," she said. "It was necessary for my soul to empty itself on paper."[7] Above all, though, she wrote because God commanded it. "Write, write, if you want to give Me glory," he told her. Conchita hesitated, saying, "I am afraid to neglect my duties." Jesus reassured her, "If I saw it thus, I would not bid you do it."[8] Just as there was no conflict between Conchita's marriage to Jesus and to Pancho, there was no conflict between her vocation as a writer and her vocation as a wife and mother.

So write she did, for decades. The intellectual labor of Concepción Cabrera de Armida resulted in nearly fifty books (including a sixty-six-volume spiritual autobiography) and about eighteen thousand pages of correspondence; this rivals the output of St. Thomas Aquinas and dwarfs that of most Doctors of the Church.

While Edith was a researcher, looking outside herself in order to be illuminated by the wonders of the philosophical and natural worlds, Conchita was enlightened from within, a mystic whose experience of the divine wasn't purely a matter of images, allegories, and feelings but of profound theological truths. In her writings, she reflected on the revelation of God's eternity and omnipotence, on the nature of God, who revealed himself to Conchita as he

---

6. *Conchita: A Mother's Spiritual Diary*, ed. Marie-Michel Philipon (New York: Alba House, 1978), http://www.apcross.org/conchita/diary.htm.

7. Luis M. Martínez, *To Be Jesus Crucified: Retreat Directed by Archbishop Luis M. Martínez* (New York: St Pauls, 2013), 11.

8. *Conchita*.

had to Moses: as "I Am" (Exod. 3:14). He spoke to her of his Incarnation and of the relationship among the persons of the Trinity. And every observation Conchita made on these topics was theologically impeccable, despite her very basic theological education.

In Conchita, the life of the Spirit stemmed from an intellectual life that was itself the gift of the Spirit. Though she was entirely unaware of the doctrine of divine generation (that the Son is eternally begotten of the Father), it was revealed to her in prayer. "I did not know there had been in God a generation," she wrote of this revelation. "I had never thought about it. An eternal Generation! A divine Generation! Oh, if I could express all that I feel in these words, which left their traces in my memory and in my heart. The impression I felt and experienced then about this divine generation was so vivid that I still tremble at the thought and become as it were mute."[9] For Conchita, reflecting on the nature of God himself (the very exercise that is the intellectual discipline of theology) drew her heart ever deeper into prayer and wonder at the goodness of God.

"I have written," Conchita muses, "on things so elevated that I do not understand them myself, for instance on the Word, on the Holy Spirit, on spiritual effects, etc. They affirmed that there was no variance with the teachings and doctrine of the Holy Church which I love more than my life and to which I want to submit myself without reservation, with all my heart."[10] Indeed, Conchita was adamant in insisting that she was no scholar, particularly when questioned about her spiritual writings. But her work makes it clear that she was a woman of great intelligence, however unschooled on the finer points of theology. This lack of formal education was no barrier for a God who desired that Conchita be a great intellectual shining light, so he taught her himself and then taught the world through a wife, mother, widow, and grandmother. This mystical prayer that touched both mind and heart strengthened Conchita through the loss of her husband when she was only thirty-nine and through the tragic deaths of three of her young sons. For all

---

9. *Conchita.*
10. *Conchita.*

she suffered, Conchita knew she was loved. She knew the one who loved her. And even in her devastating grief, that was enough.

Conchita insisted that all her words and all her wisdom came from Christ alone, causing one to wonder if perhaps she was little more than a secretary taking dictation. But in the passages where Conchita wrote her own reflections we see a genius that comes from within, as she speaks of prisms refracting light and refers over and again to the atom.[11] It's clear that God spoke to her not merely as one who would record a message but as a woman of great wisdom and intelligence whose mystical experiences would bear further fruit through her pondering of these revelations. For Conchita, the work of the intellect was never an end but rather a means to a deeper knowledge of God; through that experience of God, she wasn't stolen away from her family but returned to them refreshed and ready to love them better than before. This mother of many became more herself through the life of the mind, as well as more Christ's, more her husband's, and more her children's. This is the gift of the intellectual life for a wife and mother, indeed for any woman: it nourishes our souls so that we might nourish those we love.

Both Faith and Reason

There are, without a doubt, women in the annals of holiness for whom the intellectual life was not a driving force in their pursuit of holiness, saints for whom it was enough simply to love God without attempting to know him beyond the simple ways he had revealed himself to them. St. Agatha Kim A-gi, for example, became a saint though she was unable even to learn the Our Father. It was the simplicity of St. Bernadette Soubirous that testified to the truth of the apparitions at Lourdes—those who examined her knew that such a one as Bernadette could never have invented such a story. And countless thousands of uneducated women have loved God radically without ever analyzing the original Greek of a Scripture passage or pondering the

11. *Conchita*.

manner of the procession of the Spirit. They have loved the Theotokos without considering the meaning of that title and have given glory to God just as much as the Doctors of the Church who preached his name with such eloquence.

But the very first Christian woman pondered the things of God in her heart. She wrote poetry so majestic that it's recited daily throughout the world. She used her mind, as a woman of prayer and as the Mother of God. And while there are as yet only four female Doctors of the Church, there have always been women seeking God through the life of the mind, women who couldn't have attained holiness had they not embraced both faith and reason. For St. Edith Stein, it was a PhD in philosophy that led her to the faith. For Bl. Concepción Cabrera de Armida, it was unshakeable devotion to daily prayer that led her to a profound understanding of theology. For us, it may be an academic degree, a research project, a stack of books on the bedside table, a novel written in the margins of life, or a commitment to Scripture study that goes beyond skimming that Sunday's Gospel. It may be study that leads us to God and it may be God who leads us to study. But whatever the order, the end result of running after God in prayer and study can only be greater joy and peace, deeper faith, and stronger hope, whatever we might suffer.

Holy Boldness and the Feminine Mind

Rachel Harkins Ullmann

Recently, I was doing some research on the number of female saints while trying to write a Litany of Female Saints[1] (since there wasn't one in popular circulation). This research took me down a rabbit hole of debates over the validity of the canonization process in past eras and how a true number of male vs. female saints couldn't be calculated. Laying the debate aside, I began to notice that the odds for canonization were not in favor of women, let alone lay working mothers like myself. In discussing the intellectual life for Catholic women, you may look at a Litany of Saints and struggle with the thought that you are not represented in this list, especially if you are a lay working mother. And then, taking a closer look at the Doctors of the Church—one of the highest titles bestowed upon the saints—out of a total of thirty-six Doctors of the Church, four of them are women, equaling approximately 11 percent. Only one of the thirty-six Doctors of the Church—St. Catherine of Siena—was a layperson.

It's important to recognize how beautiful, sacred, and lengthy of a process it is to canonize a holy person. I currently serve on the canonization guild for Servant of God Mother Mary Lange, and her cause has been open since 1991. For St. Hildegard of Bingen, it took eight hundred years before she was recognized formally by the Church for her sanctity! This isn't a trivial

---

1. "Women on Mission," The GIVEN Institute website, https://giveninstitute.com/women-on-mission/.

pursuit; obtaining sanctity is difficult in and of itself, and it's even harder to provide evidence of a holy life through divine miracles as reviewed by the Congregation for the Causes of Saints in the Vatican!

So, can sainthood be achieved by a lay working woman who is pursuing an intellectual life? I serve as the executive director of The GIVEN Institute, where I work with young adult Catholic women who are seeking to use their gifts in service of the Gospel. The average woman who applies to attend the GIVEN Forum is a lay, single woman in the workplace. Women in this demographic regularly share with me that they often feel lost and like their gifts aren't wanted by the Church, or at least not until they commit to a husband or a religious order. There is a growing number of highly educated, talented young adult women who are looking to make this period of their lives fruitful and purposeful, who want to know that their gifts are needed.

When Amy Coney Barrett underwent hearings to evaluate her ability to hold the position of Supreme Court Justice, she was placed on the world stage for public scrutiny. As a Catholic wife and mother of seven, Amy was asked some unique questions. NPR published a piece detailing questions Barrett was asked that her male counterparts on the bench have never been asked during a senate judiciary meeting. "You don't have a magic formula for how you do it and handle all the children and your job and your work and your thought process, which is obviously excellent, do you?" She answered, "It's improv." "It's a sincere question. I'm genuinely curious. Who does laundry in your house?"[2]

These questions are very difficult to casually laugh off in light of my own experiences of discrimination in the workplace. Often our secular culture—and even Church culture—can stunt a woman's growth in the intellectual life.

In my own Catholic professional career, I have had to file for disability to receive a percentage of my income after first using up all my paid time off when I gave birth to my children. Paid parental leave was not offered at the archdiocese where I spent twelve years of my career. I've been denied

2. "Amy Coney Barrett Faces Gendered Questions from Senate Judiciary Committee," NPR website, October 15, 2020, https://www.npr.org/2020/10/15/924150172/amy-coney-barrett-faces-gendered-questions-from-senate-judiciary-committee.

a pumping room at a Catholic school, asked by my supervisor if I'm done having children, and told that my résumé was too erratic because I moved jobs so I could find more flexible work arrangements for my family life. I've also been privy to parish finance council meetings where raises were not given to women because "they are not the breadwinners."

A triumph in my Catholic professional career, but also a tale of how far we have to go to support lay working mothers, took place in 2018, when I negotiated a partially remote work schedule so that I could be more present to my children a few days a week. I was told by my supervisor not to tell anyone that we had made this arrangement because the other women in the office would be jealous. I now have three children, ages six and under, and run a national nonprofit from my home office. For the first time in my Catholic professional career, I don't feel that I have to apologize for being a mother or hold off on informing my supervisor of a pregnancy for fear of disappointment.

When I reflect on my own pursuit of holiness and service to the Church, there have been many challenges. I found myself questioning my place in the Church and in the world and how I was expected to use my gifts. Is the intellectual life an option for me? Does the Church value my unique and unrepeatable gifts? The answer is yes, and the answer comes directly from the Church herself!

In *Christifideles Laici*, written by Pope St. John Paul II on the Vocation and Mission of the Lay Faithful in the Church and in the World, the laity are reminded of the universal call to holiness. John Paul pays particular attention to women in this apostolic exhortation and asks all to "acknowledge the indispensable contribution of women to the building up of the Church and the development of society." He exhorts women to take up leadership roles, saying, "If anyone has this task of advancing the dignity of women in the Church and society, *it is women themselves*, who must recognize their responsibility as leading characters."[3]

---

3. Pope John Paul II, *Christifideles Laici* 49, post-synodal apostolic exhortation, December 30, 1988, vatican.va (emphasis added).

Women's participation in the intellectual life is critical for the future of the Church. Without the impact of the feminine genius in all sectors of society, the Church and the world will be deprived of the unique and unrepeatable gifts that are given to each woman due to her capacity to bear human life within her. Women, by the very nature of their *being*, work to ensure that both the economy and society treasure the family, protect the vulnerable, and keep the person at the heart of all their enterprises.

But this great gift of femininity is often overlooked if not discarded. Even John Paul II said in his *Meditation on Givenness* that "a long road led me to discover the genius of woman, and Providence itself saw to it that the time eventually came when I really recognized it and was even, as it were, dazzled by it."[4] This beloved saint admitted that it took a long time to discover the feminine genius and truly value its worth. This realization bore fruit in much of his work, which continued to uphold the dignity of femininity, especially in his "Letter to Women" and *Mulieris Dignitatem*. These writings are essential elements to the Church's teachings and to the world.

Pope St. Paul VI was also a great champion of the vital role of women. He prophesied at the close of the Second Vatican Council about the mark women would make upon the Church and the world when he said, "But the hour is coming, in fact has come, when the vocation of woman is being achieved in its fullness, the hour in which woman acquires in the world an influence, an effect and a power never hitherto achieved."[5]

Three years later, Paul VI wrote *Humanae Vitae*, which I believe to be the most important encyclical of the twentieth and—dare I say—twenty-first centuries. *Humanae Vitae* firmly and lovingly shared with the world that the Catholic Church was going to maintain its teachings on artificial contraception and that the sexual act between a man and woman must always be both unitive and procreative.

---

4. Pope John Paul II, *A Meditation on Givenness* 5, *Communio: International Catholic Review* website, February 8, 1994, https://www.communio-icr.com/files/jpii41-4.pdf.
5. Pope Paul VI, "Address of Pope Paul VI to Women," December 8, 1965, vatican.va.

While the world may have reacted to *Humanae Vitae* with disgust and felt that this was another sign of the Church being oppressive to women, Paul VI was truly freeing women to embrace the creative and generative gift within themselves, the gift of being able to knit new life within their very wombs. Women are free to embrace their maternity as integral to their feminine genius, not in opposition to it.

In 1970, this great man continued to impact Catholic women by bestowing the title of Doctor of the Church upon the first females to receive the title: St. Teresa of Avila and St. Catherine of Siena. St. Teresa of Avila was a leader, an administrator, and a breadwinner. Her choice to follow God's call upon her life to reform the Carmelite order was already risky, and asking the Carmelite General if she could extend the reform to men was an unheard-of request. Cunningly, Teresa knew she needed the support of the monks to help move things forward in the traditional Spanish culture of the time. Obviously, Teresa was pushing the cultural boundaries for women at that point in history. She oversaw the purchase of a new facility to house the sisters during this entire overhaul, much to the chagrin of the local townspeople, who were uncomfortable with her boldness. Using her intelligence, influence, and initiative, she not only offered her life as a gift for God but impacted generations to come.

St. Catherine of Siena also has a risk-taking story that can inspire any woman to be more bold in the use of her gifts.[6] From the very beginning of her journey into religious life, she was told that she didn't fit the mold. Catherine received her vocational calling at the age of sixteen, but the order that she wished to join, the Sisters of Penance, would not accept her, believing it was improper for a girl of marriageable age to take up their work. They served the poor in the city streets and typically accepted mature widows who had already fulfilled the demands of marriage and family life. Catherine was told to fulfill those expectations of a woman's role in society first before considering entering religious life. But Catherine persisted and was eventually accepted as a lay Dominican.

---

6. Terry Polakovic, *Women of Hope: Doctors of the Church* (Huntington, IN: Our Sunday Visitor, 2021), 73–74.

As she lived out her religious vocation she drew many followers, both male and female, which was unheard of in that time. She is known to have written a letter to the pope asking for his written approval of her work because "many of our citizens and their wives and also some of the nuns of my own order are quite scandalized by all the journeys—too many, they say—I have hitherto made to one place and another. [They] say that it is not right for a religious virgin to travel about so much [and with so many followers]."[7] Catherine was making waves in society and people were taking notice and questioning these traditional roles of women in the Church and the world. To cap off her remarkable influence, the pope and St. Catherine had many more conversations, including her bold request for him to return to Rome, the rightful home for the papacy—one which he eventually heeded.

In addition to Sts. Teresa and Catherine, the other two female Doctors of the Church, St. Thérèse of Lisieux and St. Hildegard of Bingen, embody the feminine genius and model for *all* women true boldness and femininity, paving the way for our own pursuits of the intellectual life. John Paul II announced St. Thérèse of Lisieux as a Doctor of the Church in 1997. After coining the phrase "feminine genius" and calling for a "new feminism" in his beautiful writings, it's no surprise that John Paul II was the pope to bestow this highest honor upon Thérèse. What may surprise many is that Thérèse is known for her "little way" and for being particularly humble. However, the story of her one trip to Rome showcases her inspirational boldness.

Thérèse, too, was not going to be accepted into a religious order because of her young age, and she decided to petition all the way up to the pope. As she and many other pilgrims approached the pope on his throne to kiss his hand, she acted in quite a different manner. She describes the moment in her autobiography, saying, "Instead of kissing it, I joined my own and lifting tear-filled eyes to his face, I cried out, 'Most Holy Father, I have a great favor to ask you! . . . Holy Father, in honor of your Jubilee, permit me to enter Carmel at the age of fifteen!'"[8]

---

7. Polakovic, 82.
8. Thérèse of Lisieux, *Story of a Soul: The Autobiography of St. Thérèse of Lisieux* (Washington, DC: ICS Publications, 1975), 134–135.

Many may ask where this holy boldness came from, especially in a time when women had very limited leadership roles in society. I believe that it came from her mother, St. Zélie Martin. Zélie was a lay working woman who owned a lace-making business. In fact, her business was so successful that her husband, St. Louis Martin, sold his watch business to support Zélie in running it. Many working mothers struggle with the balance of a home life and a professional life, and Zélie can be a model to all. Reading Thérèse's autobiography, *Story of a Soul*, I was struck by the deep relationship Thérèse had with her mother. Zélie was no less present as a mother to Thérèse while running a successful business, and that was back in the nineteenth century!

Pope Benedict XVI announced St. Hildegard of Bingen as a Doctor of the Church in 2012, making her the first female Doctor of the Church named in the twenty-first century. Hildegard was a well-rounded woman— chemist, botanist, naturalist, poet, hymnist, mystic, and abbess. She was known as the most remarkable woman of her era and said that men had made such a mess of things that "God had to call a weak woman in to save the day."[9]

My favorite story about Hildegard was when she moved her sisters out of the monastery shared with the monks.[10] This proved to be an impending financial disaster to the men who had handsomely profited from the dowries the women brought with them upon entering the monastery. What boldness for Hildegard to follow the promptings of the Holy Spirit and leave! She then served as a general contractor overseeing the building of a new monastery for her sisters modeled on the *Rule* of St. Benedict.

I have great hope reading the lives of the saints, especially of these four female Doctors of the Church, who lived with holy boldness and are now recognized as great spiritual teachers. I encourage everyone to read more about these women, pray to them, and befriend them. They will not disappoint you. I believe that very soon more women, including lay women, will be canonized and honored as Doctors of the Church. John Paul II's

9. Polakovic, *Women of Hope*, 177.
10. Polakovic, 181.

encouragement in *Christifideles Laici* for women to recognize themselves as leading characters wasn't a mere suggestion but rather the recognition of our responsibility to the Church and the world!

A popular secular feminist mantra says that "well-behaved women seldom make history." However, what many don't know is that phrase was written by Harvard professor and mother of five Laurel Thatcher Ulrich. The quotation comes from her 1976 scholarly article about little-studied Puritan funeral services and the eulogies given for females during that era.

Here is the true context of the quote: "Cotton Mather called them 'the hidden ones.' They never preached or sat in a deacon's bench. Nor did they vote or attend Harvard. Neither, because they were virtuous women, did they question God or the magistrates. They prayed secretly, read the Bible through at least once a year, and went to hear the minister preach even when it snowed. Hoping for an eternal crown, they never asked to be remembered on earth. And they haven't been. Well-behaved women seldom make history."[11]

Ulrich admits that she has been stunned by the reaction and pop-culture phenomenon surrounding her words. She commented, "My objective was not to lament their oppression, but to give them a history. . . . When I wrote that 'well-behaved women seldom make history,' I was making a commitment to help recover the lives of otherwise obscure women."[12] Just let that sink in! Were there not more great female spiritual teachers living saintly lives over the past two thousand years of Church history? Why are only 11 percent of the Doctors of the Church women? Like Ulrich, rather than lamenting what may be deemed as oppression, I write today to encourage the next generation of Catholic female leaders to rise up with holy boldness and be remembered for discovering the gift only you can give, because of the gift that you are. Pope Francis exhorts the Church to be "a listening Church" in the area of women's equality and says that by doing so the Church can "support the call to respect women's rights, and offer convinced support for greater reciprocity

11. Laurel Thatcher Ulrich, *Well-Behaved Women Seldom Make History* (New York: Alfred A. Knopf, 2007), xxviii.
12. Ulrich, xxviii, xxxiii.

between males and females, while not agreeing with everything some feminist groups propose."[13]

One of my favorite romantic comedies is *The Holiday* starring Kate Winslet. She is suffering a recent heartbreak and cannot identify her self-worth as a beloved daughter of God. She accepts a dinner invitation from an elderly neighbor named Arthur, who tells her that in the old Hollywood movies there is always a leading lady and a best friend. He says that Kate Winslet is behaving like the best friend rather than shining as the leading lady that she is meant to be. And Kate responds, "You're so right. You're supposed to be the leading lady of your own life. . . . I've been going to a therapist for three years, and she's never explained anything to me that well. That was brilliant. Brutal, but brilliant."

So take a little inspiration and advice from Paul VI, John Paul II, Benedict XVI, Francis, Teresa of Avila, Catherine of Siena, Thérèse of Lisieux, Hildegard of Bingen, Laurel Thatcher Ulrich, and even Arthur in *The Holiday*, and be the leading lady of your own life! And who knows? Maybe you will be the next female Doctor of the Church.

---

13. Pope Francis, *Christus Vivit* 42, post-synodal apostolic exhortation, March 25, 2019, vatican.va.

Intellectual Life:
From Theory to Practice

Jackie Francois Angel

There is no such thing on earth as an uninteresting subject; the only thing that can exist is an uninterested person.[1]

—G.K. CHESTERTON, *HERETICS*

From a young age, humans are filled with an exuberant desire "to know." My five-year-old and seven-year-old daughters are constantly asking questions, from the predictable "Why? Why?" to the profound "How could God create his own mother?" or "What is a 'human'?" As an evangelist, I love answering these questions and having discussions with my children. It's beautiful to see my own children hunger for the truth with wide eyes and a desire to answer the basic questions of life ("Why am I here? What am I made for? Am I loved?") without even knowing the reason why they're asking.

In my own life—when I had a deep conversion in my Catholic faith at eighteen years of age—I wanted to know why I was Catholic. I started reading everything I could get my hands on—apologetics, theology, spiritual books, papal encyclicals, and of course Scripture and the *Catechism of the Catholic Church*. I didn't want to be Catholic just because my mom was Catholic. I wanted to have reasons for my beliefs and know the "why" behind

---

1. G.K. Chesterton, *Heretics* (New York: John Lane, 1919), 38.

the "what" of each teaching of the faith. I also needed to be able to defend my faith from the onslaught of questions from belittling fellow college students who saw my Jesus T-shirts and then found out I was Catholic. "Why do you worship Mary? Why do you go to confession to a priest? Why do you believe the pope is infallible?" With all the predictable questions coming my way, I was able to engage in spirited conversations as well as continue to foster my own formation by continued study.

One of my favorite books in the early part of my conversion was St. Thérèse of Lisieux's *Story of a Soul*. St. Thérèse's "little way" constantly encouraged and reminded me to be like a little child in regards to innocence, purity of heart, awe, wonder, and most of all humility. One of the roots of humility is *humus*, which means "earth." Since humility is often seen as the foundation of all the virtues, it would make sense that the "good soil" on which the seed falls in the parable of the sower in Matthew 13 is actually a "humble heart"—a heart that is so "down to earth" that it will always grow, learn, and bear much fruit.

This is especially true in the intellectual life. St. Thérèse of Lisieux is a Doctor of the Church, yet she did not have a PhD or a master's degree. She was simply a humble disciple who was hungry to know the truth, beauty, and goodness of God. One of her favorite books was Thomas à Kempis' *The Imitation of Christ*. In his book, Thomas à Kempis repeatedly denounces the pompous intellectual who knows everything about God in his mind but does not know God in his heart.

"Every man naturally desires knowledge; but what good is knowledge without fear of God? Indeed a humble rustic who serves God is better than a proud intellectual who neglects his soul to study the course of the stars. . . . Intellectuals like to appear learned and to be called wise. Yet there are many things the knowledge of which does little or no good to the soul, and he who concerns himself about other things than those which lead to salvation is very unwise."[2]

---

2. Thomas à Kempis, *The Imitation of Christ* (Oak Harbor, WA: Faithlife, 1996), 3.

For me, the key phrase from that paragraph is *proud* intellectual. What if a "humble rustic," as Thomas à Kempis calls it, was also a *humble* intellectual? What if those of us who are missionaries, stay-at-home moms, retirees, consecrated women, working women, single women, etc. took great care to form our intellectual life not because it helped us attain degrees but because it helped us to know God and deepen our humanity, which, in turn, would help us rightly love ourselves and others?

While we absolutely need professional intellectuals who have master's degrees and PhDs and teach in universities and write academic books and articles, we must not be persuaded into thinking that because we are not reading to attain a degree our intellect is not worth forming. On the contrary, every single disciple is called to grow continually in the intellectual life. Not only would this create great saints in each one of us, but it would, in turn, create more saints in those who surround us. While a professional intellectual may tell us *about* God, we desperately need people who profoundly *know* God (and hopefully there are many professional intellectuals who can do that too). Not every disciple needs a PhD, but every disciple needs the truth, beauty, and goodness of God to dwell in his or her heart, mind, body, and soul.

St. Anselm's motto was "faith seeking understanding." As I have experienced firsthand, an encounter with God and the result of increased faith drives and compels the desire to understand that faith in its fullness. While humans are innately wired to discover and know basic facts like how to survive and how to interact with other humans, faith brings in a supernatural dimension that taps into our deepest desires and longings for things "not of this world." While I am constantly learning new skills and researching things like "how to fix a leaky toilet" or "how to bake cinnamon rolls from scratch" or "how to apply under-eye concealer to 'mature skin'" or circling down the never-ending rabbit hole of "interesting subjects" on YouTube, I must admit that all these facts and skills are not necessarily forming my intellectual life nor my spiritual life.

Is this not one of the intellectual dilemmas of today? With social media outlets like YouTube and Instagram and Twitter, we are consuming information at a great pace. With search engines like Google, we have a world of information at our fingertips. Yet it seems that a lot of this (mostly useless) information goes in one ear and out the other. But even if the information stays between my ears, is it really a formation of my intellectual life that I know who the latest celebrity is dating or what the latest dance trends are on TikTok?

In the foreword for *The Intellectual Life* by A.G. Sertillanges, James V. Schall explains that "an intellectual life, a contemplative life is itself filled with activity, but activity that is purposeful, that wants to know, and to know the truth."[3] Thus, the intellectual life is not just consuming facts and spitting them back out, nor is it knowing and learning basic skills. A true intellectual life is a desire for the truth (and beauty and goodness). I would postulate that this kind of knowledge also breeds wisdom and helps form not only the mind but also the soul. Whatever our state in life, this formation proves to be of utmost importance.

When I was in college and then a single, full-time working gal, I would have seven books on my nightstand at a time, reading (mostly theology or spiritual) books in coffee shops, planes, on the beach—wherever I could have quiet time. My intellectual life helped spur on my spiritual life. I found saints to be my mentors, and their wisdom was inspiring and convicting. Now, as a part-time-working, homeschooling mom of four kids ages seven and younger, my energy is much lower and my time is much thinner. It seems sometimes that space for the intellectual life is allocated haphazardly. It has to fit in wherever I can fit it. Gone are the days when I can read seventy pages (or a whole book!) in one sitting, and now I rarely finish two sentences before being interrupted by a delightful child of mine. I almost laughed out loud when reading this part of *The Intellectual Life*, which shares a schedule by which to get your intellectual life going: "In order to keep this time for

---

3. James V. Schall, foreword to A.G. Sertillanges, *The Intellectual Life: Its Spirit, Conditions, Methods*, trans. Mary Ryan (Washington, DC: The Catholic University of America Press, 1998), xii.

your work and to keep it really free, rise punctually and promptly; breakfast lightly; avoid futile conversations, useless calls, limit your correspondence to what is strictly necessary; gag the newspapers! These rules, which we have given as a general safeguard for the life of study, apply most of all to its intense hours."[4]

Avoid futile conversations, you say? My seven-year-old and five-year-old girls are fighting (and possibly crying) over who has the authority to make the rules to the game they're playing and it's only 7:30 a.m. Limit your correspondence, hmm? My one-and-a-half-year-old toddler is bleating like a baby goat, "Mom, mom, moooooooooom!" while my three-year-old son is shouting, "I have poo poos!" It's comical because it's true and it's real life.

No matter which stage of life we are in—single, married, or consecrated—there will always be distractions and roadblocks to forming the intellectual life. But there are immense benefits to the intellectual life that must not be overlooked. Zena Hitz, in her book *Lost in Thought: The Hidden Pleasures of an Intellectual Life*, has many profound statements regarding "why" the intellectual life is necessary for humanity, but here are four she mentions that are too good not to share:

—It is a form of the inner life of a person, a place of retreat and reflection.

—As such it is *withdrawn from the world*, where 'the world' is understood in its (originally Platonic, later Christian) sense as the locus of competition and struggle for wealth, power, prestige, and status.

—It is a source of *dignity* . . .

—It opens space for *communion*: it allows for profound connection between human beings.[5]

---

4. Sertillanges, 95.

5. Zena Hitz, *Lost in Thought: The Hidden Pleasures of an Intellectual Life* (Princeton, NJ: Princeton University Press, 2020), 56.

I needed these four things as much when I was single as I do now as a wife and mom. When I was single, my alone reading time allowed me to be creative. My second singer-songwriter album "Divine Comedy" came into being while reading Dr. Peter Kreeft's *Three Philosophies of Life*, which, like Dante's *Divine Comedy*, goes from hell to purgatory to heaven. As a mom, my alone reading time (albeit much shorter) allows me to regain some sanity and solitude from the constant (sometimes delightful and sometimes not-so-delightful) noise of children. As a single woman, I absolutely needed connection with friends to share ideas and vulnerability while always reminding me that I wasn't alone. As a married woman, I not only have built-in community with my husband, but I also have many adult female friends offering a respite of mature conversation after a day of singing "Wheels on the Bus" to my toddler.

As women, whether we consider ourselves academic or not, there is a need for our "feminine genius" in the world. Not only do we form our intellect for our own growth, dignity, and inner life, but we also form our minds to lead others to the true, good, and beautiful. As Pope St. John Paul II said in his "Letter to Women," women have a special insight that helps "enrich the world's understanding and [helps] to make human relations more honest and authentic."[6] His term "feminine genius" includes sensitivity, intuitiveness, generosity, and fidelity as four noble characteristics that women specifically bring into the world to help it grow to be more human. I can most definitely say that my "feminine genius" married with an intellectual life has helped me become a better wife, mother, friend, and woman of God. Whether it has been Scripture, a spiritual book, or a parenting book, I have learned how to be more understanding, more tender, more vulnerable, more patient, more human.

One recent experience of this has been with my very sensitive and very passionate (another way of saying "someone who has meltdowns that mirror demonic possession") five-year-old daughter. Because her temperament is so different from that of her elder sister, my "feminine genius" of sensitivity and

---

6. Pope John Paul II, "Letter of Pope John Paul II to Women" 2, June 29, 1995, vatican.va.

intuitiveness realized I had to discipline and teach her differently. Thus, I sought different books and advice on how to deal with such a child. In learning these things, I relayed to my husband how we as parents should change our parenting style with her. I could tell intuitively that while our eldest daughter has a strong need for words of affirmation (see Gary Chapman's *Five Love Languages*) and thus receives discipline easily (because she is more prone to people-pleasing and doesn't want to disappoint us), our second daughter is very emotionally sensitive and has a strong need for physical touch (and so, as a result, will fly off the handle when sent to a "time-out"). When I realized that she needed a physical hug and touch quickly after being sent to "time-out," it changed everything. That touch reassured her immensely. My encouraging her that I love her even when she behaves poorly melted her tense and anxious body.

I am still learning a great deal about my children—how to raise and form them into saints according to their temperament, how to teach them based on what is appropriate for their age, and how to love them warmly. But I am also still learning how to form myself—how to allow space for my own spiritual and intellectual growth, which types of information help me grow as a person, and which types of knowledge de-form my humanity. I am still learning how to be a "humble, rustic intellectual" who doesn't need to pursue an academic degree to motivate my pursuit of the intellectual life. You may be working on this, too, and that is honorable. What is non-negotiable is that you, as a woman and disciple of God, are needed in this world—your curiosity and wonder, your creativity, your peacefulness, your wisdom and knowledge, your humanity. In a word, your feminine genius. So, be not afraid to form your intellectual life.

Becoming a Bibliophile

Haley Stewart

We read to know we're not alone.
—*SHADOWLANDS*

The intellectual life is a continuing conversation. In conversation with God in prayer, he speaks truth to our hearts. In conversation with his creation, we cultivate our minds by reflecting on the beauty around us. And in conversation with others, we learn from their insights what we had not yet discovered ourselves. In other words, no woman is an island. Human beings are relational, and the intellectual life is relational too.

We learn and grow in this relational dialogue, but our conversation with others isn't limited to the people we can speak to in the same room. Through the gift of books we can "speak" with others through pages written on the other side of the world hundreds of years ago. We can experience a dialogue that transcends geographic and chronological distance. We can have a conversation that feeds our hearts, minds, and souls.

I have never been a particularly orderly person. The habit of leaving my things out everywhere was clear to my longsuffering mother very early on. By age five I was both a devoted reader and decidedly untidy. I remember my mother sighing as she picked up yet another book left askew, probably noting a damaged spine from being left open on my messy bedroom floor, and begging me, "Please be more careful, Haley. Books are our *friends*." The older I get, the more truth I see in her words. Books are our friends. As the character of C.S. Lewis in the biographical film *Shadowlands* says, "We read to know we're not alone." We are kept company by the bookish voices that guide us on our journey.

But not everyone falls in love with reading as a child or develops a habit of conversing with these friends made of paper and ink. And even those of us who do read as children might fall away from those practices during certain busy seasons of life and need to cultivate them anew. I've co-hosted a bookish podcast for Catholic women over the past several years, and one of the most frequent questions we get from listeners is how to make time to read. "How do you do it?" they ask. "How do you fit it in?" This is a struggle most of us relate to—we lead busy lives! But it's never too late to become a reader.

Like other priorities, our reading life will ebb and flow depending on the season. A new job, new baby, medical emergency, or big move can understandably affect our reading habits. There will be times we read less and times we read more. But after a demanding season of life we might find ourselves stuck in a rut, not knowing how to begin again. How do we make new "friends" or revive our company with old ones? How do we make time for a reading life? How do we become lovers of books—bibliophiles?

Like any habit, reading is a practice that requires intentionality. We have to build it into our daily schedule. Can you wake up early to spend some time in your favorite chair reading and sipping coffee as the sun rises? Do you prefer to settle in with a good book after dinner? Could an audiobook keep you company on your commute? Can you sneak in twenty minutes of reading while sitting in the school pickup car line? Can you trade out your evening TV shows for a novel? There are creative ways to weave books into your life, although how we incorporate reading into our days isn't going to look the same for everyone.

But whatever plan you engage to help you read more, don't let the perfect be the enemy of the good. A few minutes here and there is always better than nothing at all. Our days may be packed, but there are often spaces we fill with distractions like social media. What if instead we filled those moments with books? As author Tasha Tudor wrote in a passage about the dignity of quotidian tasks, "When you're stirring the jam you can read Shakespeare."[1] There's nothing to stop you from listening to an audiobook while you exercise or reading a novel as you wait for a doctor's appointment. Make good use of those in between moments!

A Note on Reading Mothers

While mothers are by no means the only women who find themselves with heavy demands on their time, cultivating a reading life as a mother (especially during baby and toddler years) can feel impossible. My first child was born soon after I graduated from a rigorous and intellectually stimulating undergraduate program. In just a few months I went from a heavy fare of the great texts of the Western tradition to an exclusively baby board book diet. I had a colicky baby and was too exhausted from new motherhood to read any of "my" books for ages. I remember finally diving into a good book for the first time postpartum (*Jonathan Strange & Mr. Norrell* by Susanna Clarke—a delicious fantasy) and realizing how much I'd missed my friendship with books.

While it may be unreasonable to expect to read as much during the high intensity years of parenting as in other times of life, you can still be a bibliophile. Mothers are people. And they deserve a chance to read like everyone else. If that requires an hour or two away at a coffee shop once a week to read a good novel, moms should be able to ask for that time guilt-free.

The early years of parenthood can be particularly tough on reading time, but as children get older, books can become a family affair. During the lockdowns of the COVID-19 pandemic, I realized that we all needed a built-in daily reading hour to stay sane. We made a plan for when it would happen each day and carried stacks of books and quilts out to the front yard to read in the sunshine. My kids preferred to find a good tree to climb with a

---

1. Tasha Tudor and Richard Brown, *The Private World of Tasha Tudor* (New York: Little, Brown and Company, 1992), 104.

lofty reading perch. I would read my books, they would read theirs. Reading hour is now a steady, cultivated daily habit, going strong after almost two years. It's taken hard work to cultivate this habit in family life, but it's a gift to us all!

Reading to Grow

Few pleasures in life compare to being immersed in a compelling page-turner! It is good for reading to delight us, and there's certainly nothing wrong with reading for entertainment or even just for comfort (I re-read *Anne of Green Gables* at least once a year for that very reason). But it's also important to stretch ourselves to read for more than entertainment. To really cultivate the intellectual life, we may have to dig a little bit deeper. We will have to befriend books that push us out of our comfort zone. Reading books that challenge our minds and force us to wrestle with difficult ideas, slow down to absorb beautiful imagery, or re-read before mastering isn't for the faint of heart! And often, after matriculating from higher education, non-academics like myself can fall out of the practice of reading books that are really going to require us to grow.

One tactic to develop our intellects with good books is to reach for books in different genres than we usually gravitate to. I could happily read only modern British novels to the end of my days. While defending the brilliant merits of that genre is a hill I would die on, I need to venture beyond my darlings in order to grow. Why not branch out into philosophy, poetry, or theology? Grab a biography or a memoir? Try a classic fantasy or some science fiction? There is so much out there!

But this is easier said than done. How do we avoid getting bogged down agonizing over what title to choose? One strategy is to create a reading syllabus—created by you and for you. What books are sitting on your shelves that you've always meant to read? Write them down. Jot down classic titles that you're determined to read before you die. Take a look at what you've listed so far and then add some color. If it's mostly non-fiction, add some good novels. If it's all prose, add a collection of poetry. If it's all fiction, consider a collection of essays or a spiritual memoir. Having a self-curated reading list isn't everyone's cup of tea, but it works for many and solves the age-old question of "what will I read next?"

We'll still hit bumps on the road, of course. Perhaps one book feels impossible to finish and we drag it around for months instead of taking a break and picking up something new. (I'll often tackle multiple books at a time, so if I'm just not feeling sharp enough for a dense read, I can pick up the novel I'm working through instead.) You'll have to develop the habits that work for you. Keep a book in your purse, in the car, in every room of the house. Be able to produce one at any moment like a magician finding a coin behind a child's ear!

And to really dive into good texts, don't be shy about letting yourself be a student and making notes in your books. I will underline passages, put stars next to important sentences, write notes in the margins, or dog-ear my favorite pages. If this treatment of books sounds horrifying (and you're determined never to lend me any books to be so profaned!), writing in your books isn't the only way to study them well. Have a little notebook for keeping track of your thoughts and passages you want to return to, or use whatever method works for you.

Companions on the Way

If we are going to really get the most out of our reading lives, we must remember that the intellectual life is relational. We need other people to be companions on our journey. Reading is often considered a solitary task, but if we don't invite others in, we will not get very far. If you're getting bogged down or feeling uninspired in your reading life, create community by joining or forming a book club.

Sharing the reading life with others brings not only more depth to our experience but also more joy. In a beautiful novel about a book club formed by inhabitants of a Nazi-occupied island during World War II, *The Guernsey*

Literary and Potato Peel Pie Society, a handful of local villagers gather to discuss what they're reading. Their debates about books are spirited, and their literary community helps them survive an unimaginably difficult time. Several of the society members didn't realize their love for reading until they began to become bibliophiles together.

An in-person or online book club can offer literary community that helps us as readers. But there are other ways to build bookish community as well. If one particular book is intimidating you, chat with someone who loves it and absorb their enthusiasm—this is how I made it through *The Brothers Karamazov* after three tries. In turn, when you fall in love with a book, share it with others. Like Frodo's companions in Tolkien's *The Lord of the Rings*, we all need a fellowship to keep us on the path. Create a community that will help motivate and accompany you.

Reading Should Be a Joyful Feast

We live in a culture that focuses on productivity and measurability, and these ideals can carry over to our reading lives. For instance, there are many tools available to help you reach your goals to read a certain number of books each year. These aids can be motivating and there's certainly a place for them! But being a bibliophile is about much more than reaching measurable goals to check books off of a list. The reading life is something alive and growing like a garden, not sterile and efficient like a factory. The goal of devoting time to books isn't that we can be more productive but that we can become more human! Reading, then, should be a habit of joy and wonder. It should not feel like something we clock in to do and then clock out from with relief when we have completed our allotted reading time.

That isn't to say, of course, that reading is always immediately gratifying or that it doesn't require exertion. But if there is nothing fun about reading, we're doing it wrong. We eat to feed our bodies, we read to feed our minds— and this experience should be one of festivity. We could eat only candy, but it wouldn't bring health to our bodies. We *can* read only fluff, but it won't offer sustenance to our minds. Human beings need real nourishment to be healthy. And yet, if we forget to treat ourselves like human beings rather than machines in need of fuel, we can miss the mark. We won't thrive on an oatmeal-only diet, for instance, because we are created to *enjoy* food! In the same way, we shouldn't treat reading like drudgery. We should read books that make our hearts dance as well as ones that we know are "good for us." Imagine our reading life as a feast set before us: meaty dishes, vitamin-filled vegetables, and sustaining starchy potatoes that will stick to our ribs. But also puddings and pies! Cheese and toast! Strawberries and cream! We should joyfully savor our books, remembering that the reading life should be festive as well as nourishing and that every good meal is to be shared—with friends across the tables or in the pages of our books. Become a bibliophile. Join the feast!

An Integrated Mind and Heart

Sr. Theresa Aletheia Noble

In the first grade, I entered a Christmas poster contest at my elementary school. I had serious plans to become an artist and thought my win inevitable due to my considerable expertise in the complex art of drawing Christmas trees. Instead, a classmate's poster drew widespread acclaim throughout my small elementary school, and I ended up with a red honorable mention ribbon. Upon returning home that day, I informed my mother that my plans to become an artist were canceled. "If I cannot win an art contest in the first grade in a small elementary school," I reasoned, "the chances that I will become a successful artist are just too low, so it's not worth pursuing." My mother looked at me strangely. The expression on her face seemed to say, "I have no idea how I birthed this child characterized by such cold logic and idealistic artistic aspirations at the same time." A combination of detached, logical reasoning and heartfelt, creative idealism continues to mark my search for identity in the world. As I have prayed with this strange conflict of mind and heart, I have come to believe that aspects of it can highlight what it means to be a woman in the intellectual-creative sphere in today's world.

As hard as I tried to submerge my artistic aspirations after my first-grade failure, they reasserted themselves in a love for reading fiction and writing. My mother began to homeschool me in the third grade, and this time marked the beginning of my intellectual life. I had always enjoyed reading, but homeschooling opened large swathes of time in my day because I would finish a typical school day's work in a couple of hours. Then, after I had finished my schoolwork, I'd spend hours every afternoon reading book piles of my own choosing. Scarcely a week would go by before I would finish at least five books. I read *The Chronicles of Narnia*, *A Wrinkle in Time*, *A Girl of the Limberlost*, *Anne of Green Gables*, and every World War II–era fiction book that I could get my hands on.

By the sixth grade I had become an unabashed bibliophile. My family had moved from Ohio to Oklahoma and I had returned to school, but I would bring books with me to read in the school cafeteria amid the screams and food fights that would erupt. This did little to endear me to my fellow middle schoolers, but I was unconcerned with their approval, or, more accurately, I wanted to read more than I cared what they thought. Just as I had brought my logical, naturally philosophical mind to my fascination with World War II–era fiction in elementary school, I now brought it to dystopian novels like *1984*, *Fahrenheit 451*, and *Brave New World*. The extreme circumstances of both fictional genres helped me to explore morality and the problem of suffering. I found responses to my questions not in logical proofs but in the relationships, stories, and human experiences that were in the books I read. Fiction was a source of integration for my heart and my mind. Books helped me think through problems, developed my love for learning, initiated questions that would accompany me throughout life, and were my companions and encouragement in a world that seemed to be far too focused on the practical.

Yet no amount of literature could resolve my wrestling with the problem of suffering in my heart and mind. By the age of fourteen this struggle had become a real source of angst. Just as I had renounced art in the first grade, I felt that I had reached a logical point of no return with the problem of suffering. So I renounced God and became an atheist. However, though I had stopped wrestling explicitly with God, I continued to grapple with the problem of suffering in my reading choices—especially Dostoevsky's *Crime and Punishment*. Shot through with Christian themes, the novel took me months to read on my own in high school, but I doggedly worked through it.

I was fascinated by Raskolnikov's struggle with the evil within himself. The book raised a question I had asked myself repeatedly since I first began to read: "What keeps me from doing the evil acts that people do in these books and in real life? Am I as capable of it as they are?" I was becoming more and more convinced that the answer was yes.

During my senior year, I applied to colleges up and down the East Coast. Almost as an afterthought, I ended up attending Bryn Mawr, an all-women's college. I arrived from Oklahoma trembling and unsure and quickly found my dorm on the stately East Coast campus. As I walked among the Jacobean, Gothic-style buildings modeled after Oxford and Cambridge, I had the sense that something important and purposeful was happening within them. But I wasn't sure whether I was really meant to be one of the women who would enter their solemn doors. Above the Great Library Hall in the middle of campus, a statue of Athena with an owl perched on her shoulder towered over the door. Within the hall, several oil paintings of former college presidents lined the walls. It took me a moment to realize that what was striking about them was that the faces of so many women peered out. Though I knew that the intellectual life of women had been overshadowed by many centuries of discrimination, lack of education, and lack of resources, I nevertheless felt that day, looking at those portraits, a surge of encouragement, boldness, and wonder.

Literature seemed an obvious major. Why not dedicate all my time and attention to something I had always loved? My logical mind, however, thirsted for more explicit explorations of philosophical problems. The internal mind-heart conflict I had submerged so neatly in the first grade resurfaced once again, gasping for air. Although it came less naturally to me and inspired less passionate feelings, I ended up choosing political science as a major. Perhaps it was cold practicality; I knew it would be more helpful in finding a job after college. But I also wonder if I intuitively knew that I needed to exercise my logical mind in another way by concentrating on political philosophy. Studying political philosophy helped develop my critical thinking and, in many ways, led my previous wrestling with philosophical problems in literature onto clearer, more explicit paths. Firmly entrenched now in my plan to intellectually develop myself in a more practical way, I made plans to go to law school after college. I had taken the LSAT and had been accepted to several schools when perhaps the only one who could deter me from my plans did—God.

The spring before law school would begin in the fall, I traveled to Costa Rica to work on a farm for several months. While there, my life slowed down and I experienced the start of what would become a lifelong journey of integration between my mind and heart. A sudden conversion—from atheism to theism—then led me to believe in the One who would direct and instruct me in this journey. That day, as I walked down a quiet rural road surrounded by mountains, I went from not believing in God to believing in God in a few moments. Surrounded by the beauty of nature, God moved my mind and heart to comprehend that the beauty of the world has an uncaused cause, one that is Beauty itself. In a flash, I understood five truths that applied not only to myself but to every human being—God exists, he created me, he knows me, he loves me, and he has a plan for my life.

After I returned from Costa Rica, I began to discover God's plan for my life, and the wrestling between my mind and heart slowed more. God's grace began to bridge the chasm between my mind and heart. He began to transform me in him through my choices, my experience of prayer, and the grace of the sacraments. Rather than directing my own life, I began to look to God for answers. As I followed God's direction through prayer, my intellectual-creative life developed in ways I never would have predicted or chosen on my own. Following God's will led me to work in IT in Silicon Valley, then to vowed religious life, and later to post-graduate work in philosophy and theology. Now, my media apostolate with the Daughters of St. Paul both develops my creative, artistic heart (that I had submerged for so long) through the work of writing and exercises my logical mind through the strenuous work of editing.

Though my conversion put me on a path toward God, and in him I found a far more integrated intellectual-creative life, I will not pretend that it immediately healed my fragmented heart and mind. Even now I continue to struggle and see the wounds of fragmentation in my life. But, over time, as I have prayed with this conflict, I have realized that the roots of this battle within me are far deeper than the length of my short life. Growing up, I had absorbed the age-old stereotype that femininity is closer to the irrational than the rational. A logical artist, I quickly realized that my practical, reasonable mind was more favored by society than my intuitive heart. This realization led me to make certain choices and to reject in many ways not only my unique personality but my femininity.

As women, it's important to realize just how much we take our current status in society for granted. Women are only now (and only in some parts of the world) just emerging from centuries of having our intellectual abilities questioned and intellectual growth discouraged. For most of human history, women's intellectual capacities have been considered subordinate and inferior to men's, and even our ability to reason clearly at all has been sometimes doubted. As we are only just emerging from many centuries of suppression of the intellectual lives of women, it would be overly optimistic to assume that women operate in the intellectual-creative sphere without vestiges of the past. Thus, the continuing impact of this historical reality on our current efforts in the intellectual-creative sphere cannot be underestimated. And this context must be recognized first in order to explore what it means to be a woman in the intellectual-creative sphere today.

Interestingly, throughout history, convents were one of the few contexts in which women's intellectual growth was encouraged to some extent. Still, women in the Church—including women like St. Hildegard of Bingen and Juliana Morell—lived within a historical and ecclesial context that presumed the undervaluation of the intellectual life of women. Women's widespread participation in the intellectual life of the Church is thus still in a fairly nascent stage. Unfortunately, the potential for women's contribution to the intellectual-creative sphere and the life of the Church is often left unexplored, and attempts to articulate women's contributions fall into facile stereotypes and superficiality.

However we choose to articulate women's contributions to the intellectual-creative sphere in the Church and in the world at large, it's important to avoid what Sr. Prudence Allen describes as the "fractional" model of complementarity between women and men. This model portrays women's contributions as wedded to men's contributions and thus creating a whole. However, women's creative-intellectual life does not merely *fill in* the intellectual-creative spaces that men do not occupy. Rather, when describing the role of women in the world, the "integral complementarity" model, as described by Sr. Prudence Allen, most respects our dignity:

> The integral complementarity model . . . argues that each man and each woman is a complete person, in an ontologically important sense. When they enter into interpersonal relations, the effect is synergetic; something more happens in relationship than parts of a person adding up to one person; something new is generated.[1]

This model, applied to the intellectual-creative sphere, would recognize that women's capacities and contributions are not space fillers but complete in themselves.

Unfortunately, an integral model of complementarity between men and women seems common in neither secular nor faith contexts. In secular spheres, equality is often emphasized to the extent of ignoring women's potentially unique contributions to the intellectual life. And in some faith-based contexts, women's unique contributions can be overly emphasized and stereotyped to the point that they're *de facto* diminished. Neither of these emphases take into account the idea that often the intellectual-creative spheres in which women now find themselves, including within the Church, are characterized by a particularly male-centered way of interacting with and thinking about the world. The temptation for women can thus be to conform to these environments rather than to take risks and to participate in

---

1. Prudence Allen, "Man-Woman Complementarity: The Catholic Inspiration," *Logos: A Journal of Catholic Thought and Culture* 9, no. 3 (Summer 2006): 95. doi:10.1353/log.2006.0021.

intellectual-creative work in a uniquely feminine, integrated, and bold way.

Post-Enlightenment intellectual life, with its mind-body dualism, also does not serve women well. Unfortunately, this approach to the intellectual life has characterized the time in which women's contributions have begun to be more welcomed. This modern way of thinking often either elevates certain forms of reason above all others or reduces the heart's intuitions to sentimental affectivity and relativism. Of course, the diminution of the heart is nothing new. As Dietrich von Hildebrand pointed out, "Whereas the intellect and the will have been made the object of searching [philosophical] analysis, the phenomenon of the heart has been largely neglected."[2] This diminution of the heart and its division from the mind is far more commonplace now. And women, especially those called to the intellectual-creative life, should note how it can lead not only to fragmentation and lack of integration but also to a rejection of our natural capabilities and gifts as women.

How then can women today pursue integration so that we might more fully bring both our intellectual and creative gifts into the world? First, we can look to Scripture to see how this integration looks. Rifts between the mind and heart, for instance, are not readily apparent in scriptural images of the human person. The Hebrew version of Deuteronomy 6:5 says, "You shall love the Lord your God with all your heart, and with all your soul, and with all your strength." But in some versions of the Greek Septuagint, the word "heart" is replaced with "mind." St. Paul helps us to understand just how integrated our minds and hearts are meant to be when he writes to the Philippians, "Make my joy complete: be of the same mind, having the same love, being in full accord and of one mind" (Phil. 2:2). These passages show us how inextricably intertwined the mind and heart are truly meant to be, especially in our spiritual lives, which should always be at the foundation of our intellectual-creative work.

Philosopher Edith Stein, also known as St. Teresa Benedicta of the Cross, believed that the human and scriptural ideal of integration is one by

---

2. Dietrich von Hildebrand, *The Heart: An Analysis of Human and Divine Affectivity* (South Bend, IN: St. Augustine's Press, 2012), 135.

which woman is already particularly characterized: "The feminine species expresses a unity and wholeness of the total psychosomatic personality and a harmonious development of the faculties."[3] However, in today's world, this wholeness does not always come naturally to us as women, and so much prevents us from finding it *unless* we find it in God. Through prayer and the sacraments, God's grace unites our divided and fragmented selves in Christ, the divine Son of God who became human so that we might be drawn up into God's divine life.

When we strive to live united to Jesus, we can be sure that he will continue to integrate our minds and hearts more fully in him. Christ enables women to confidently bring our entire beings to the intellectual-creative sphere, even the parts that we might fear could be dismissed as irrational. The world needs who we are as women; it needs our emotional integration, which refines our intellectual contributions. The world needs women's minds and hearts, joined in Christ, to be like two rivers that purify one another in a unity that can only come from the One who is both Logos and Love.

---

3. Edith Stein, *Essays on Woman*, trans. Freda Mary Oben (Washington, DC: ICS Publications, 1996), 187.

Marriage, Motherhood, and the Mind

Stephanie Gray Connors

I am my father's daughter. Like him, I love books, going to bookstores, and diving into my finds. As a child, I loved to get cozy with a blanket or sit near the heat vent on the floor while engrossed in a work of literature. I'm grateful to my dad for passing on his love of learning.

My father grew up in a large Catholic family in Scotland. Life certainly had its challenges, but he was always keen to learn. Though he never went to university, he is brilliant, well-informed, and self-taught in so many areas, all because of an intentional and independent pursuit of the intellectual life. And there's a lesson here for us all: regardless of circumstance or opportunity, we should, even informally, focus on rigorous development of the intellect.

As I grew older, discussion and debate with friends and colleagues on all kinds of "hot topics" developed into a favorite pastime. I thrived when wrestling with ideas, when challenging and being challenged in the great activity of thinking. My husband and I laugh about when we first met and how our weekend was filled with intense conversations about various stimulating intellectual and spiritual topics.

What sets humans apart from other animals? Being made in God's image, we share in the attributes and features of our heavenly Father, which include his rational nature. We have the capacity to think and reason, which allows us to know truth and leads us to creativity and advancement. As someone who has a twenty-plus-year career in the intellectual arena as a speaker, debater, and author in the pro-life movement and has recently embarked on my own vocation of marriage, I ask myself, "How do I continue to foster the intellectual life, not just in my work, but quite particularly in my vocation as wife and mother?" As I reflect on this, three features come to mind:

1) A Woman Who Studies and Seeks Counsel

When I was eighteen, I met a speaker who would become one of my mentors. He would often muse about the lost art of debate. He shared that Abraham Lincoln and Stephen Douglas went on tour debating slavery in the 1800s, speaking to crowds of thousands upon thousands for hours at a time. Today, people seem more interested in following tweets of 280 characters than reading substantial content. But I encourage a return to depth. If we want to really understand a topic, we need to dive deep. We must consult experts and even welcome opposition. Listening to one person *in the context of another who disagrees* provides an opportunity for our own minds to clarify inconsistencies, fortify weaknesses, embolden strengths, and so forth.

As a wife and mother who does some work outside the home but who has also happily embraced life as a homemaker, listening to in-depth content while cleaning or cooking affords an opportunity to expand my mind while serving my family. While the tasks of a homemaker are often demeaned, I relish the monotony and know these are the perfect moments for multi-tasking. I can put on a challenging podcast or video and enrich my mind while I care for my household. In contrast, my husband's work often requires more of his attention and offers less opportunity for multi-tasking like this. This puts me as a woman in a unique position where I am afforded more time to stay on top of what's happening in the world or the Church and then share it with my spouse and others.

I am a big believer that what comes in inspires what goes out, or better yet, that one must receive in order to give. During the seasons in life when I am intentional about listening to or reading new material to expand my mind, I get more ideas that inform conversation with family and friends (whose responses then bolster my insights) or help me develop work material. Having said that, I've also found that the intellectual life is enhanced by carving out times of silence for simple contemplation (Robert Cardinal Sarah's book *The Power of Silence* is a good reminder of this) or by listening to different genres of music that also facilitate reflection.

Study is important not only in the necessity of the moment (e.g., staying on top of the news cycle or drafting an essay for class) but also in preparation for something. In 2020, I got married three weeks after my fortieth birthday, and although I wed older than most, I had spent my adult life studying for my vocation. In my twenties and thirties, there were times when I questioned whether I would ever get married and thought that perhaps I was meant to be a religious sister.

Over those two decades, I did much to develop my intellect in preparation for whatever my ultimate "Big V" vocation would be. I learned about attachment theory and how our families of origin influence our tendencies and behavior. I made many efforts to understand myself better as well as grow and change in areas that would benefit from pruning in order to ultimately serve my vocation. Annual retreats, spiritual direction, spiritual reading, organizing book studies with friends, conferences, courses, and even counseling were all part of my pursuit.

There was a time my cousin recommended I read a particular book on singleness (although I've lost count of how many on that topic I ended up consuming over the years!) and I found the author so engaging that I organized a book study of her book on marriage, inviting my married friends to learn with me even though I was yet to be living their vocation. One of the points the author espoused was the importance of respecting husbands. In fact, even St. Paul says this when he declares, "a wife should respect her husband" (Eph. 5:33). That passage is preceded by the dictate for the man to "love his wife as himself" (Eph. 5:33). It's no accident that the husband is commanded *to love* and the wife is commanded *to respect*. Men and women are different. Yes, there are similarities, but we are not identical, which makes for the beauty of *complementarity*. It's not that men do not need love or that women do not need respect; rather, it's that instead of guiding people to do that which comes most naturally to them (e.g., the nurturing nature of a woman disposes her to love so readily), we are challenged to focus on what the other needs most. Whether I was to eventually get married or become a consecrated woman under a vow of obedience to her superior, the study of respect and submission to leadership was invaluable. This, along with the other topics I studied, served me well for eventually meeting my husband. Our dating and engagement totaled less than a year. That whirlwind romance was facilitated by a lifetime of intentional and intellectual preparation.

Now that two have become one, my husband and I enjoy carving out time learning *together*, whether it's reading books that we eventually swap or diving into the Church's highest form of prayer outside the Mass—the Liturgy of the Hours. During our first Lent as a married couple, we decided to take up the practice of praying the Office of Readings daily; we chose that particular "hour" of prayer because it incorporated reflections by early Church Fathers. We wanted to learn from the insights of those oldest and closest to the time of Christ. Diving into the intellectual life together has created a habit of constantly seizing opportunities to learn—whether it's responding to a parish bulletin announcement to sign up for a course on Jesus and the Gospels, listening to educational podcasts while on road trips, or discussing Sunday readings.

I have also found it invaluable to seek mentorship. Various priests, monks, and even a lay woman have provided spiritual guidance to me over the years. The key when seeking the counsel of others is to look for the fruit in their lives, for as the Scripture says, "Every good tree bears good fruit" (Matt. 7:17). In fact, when my husband and I got pregnant, we reached out to a couple we know who have several children who are sweet, intelligent, holy, and well-behaved. We asked them for book recommendations so we could learn from the same authorities they relied on in order to raise holy children. Seeking the wisdom of holy men and women whose lives reflect virtue positions us well for our own growth in holiness.

2) A Woman Who Encourages

I love learning with my husband. I admire his strong mind and know it's a gift meant to be shared, not only with his students (it's helpful he's a professor), but with our family, friends, and myself. In fact, I credit countless conversations with him, and the profound insight he imparted, as providing core content for the book I wrote on in vitro fertilization. I am also grateful that, although I am my husband's companion, he is our leader. Embracing the attitude that I am in submission to him—"under the mission"—in no way threatens me; in fact, it encourages me. St. Paul wrote,

> Wives, be subject to your husbands as you are to the Lord. For the husband is the head of the wife just as Christ is the head of the church, *the body of which he is the Savior.* Just as the church is subject to Christ, so also wives ought to be, in everything, to their husbands. *Husbands, love your wives, just as Christ loved the church and gave himself up for her,* in order to make her holy by cleansing her with the washing of water by the word, so as to present the church to himself in splendor, without a spot or wrinkle or anything of the kind—yes, *so that she may be holy and without blemish. In the same way, husbands should love their wives as they do their own bodies.* He who loves his wife loves himself. (Eph. 5:22–28, emphasis added)

Because my husband takes his faith seriously, I know his guidance is modeled after Christ's servant leadership. As Christ laid down his life for the Church, so my husband does for our family. As Christ wants what's best for the Church, so my husband wants what's best for his family. Who wouldn't want to follow someone with that perspective? This means I want to be an encourager, not an impediment, to my husband's spiritual development so that he thrives in his leadership role.

I think, for example, of how Christ took time to leave his disciples in order to be in a quiet place and pray. He drew close to his heavenly Father, and divine life overflowed into all he did and said. That reminds me of a time my husband asked if I'd be okay with him going on a camping trip with a priest friend and other Catholic men for a night, leaving me with our three-month-old baby; I was more than happy to agree, as it would be a great opportunity for him, and the fruits of it would ultimately bless our family too. Similarly, when he and that same priest along with a group of men decided to have regular gatherings in order to study the patristics (the writings of the early Church Fathers), I wholeheartedly supported him. Fostering the intellectual life of my husband is part of my task of helping him on his journey to heaven while at the same time facilitating his role of being the best husband and father he can be. What he learns naturally overflows into teaching our family.

3) A Woman Who Embraces Hospitality as a Conduit for Compelling Conversation

I've always had a special place in my heart for priests. When I was a child, my parents were intentional about having our pastor over for dinner. As a teen, I was a youth leader, which meant working closely with my pastor. When I went to college and then graduated, I met many priests through my work who became good friends. In a time when clergy are often cast in the light of sex scandals, my experience of our shepherds has been vastly different than what the world perceives. I have been nurtured, guided, and inspired by godly men who truly live up to their clerical vocation. In fact, I am reminded of a meme I once saw that likened priests to airplanes—the few that crash make the news but most fly successfully. I know the latter.

I therefore was convicted, especially once I got married, that I wanted to make where I lived a home of hospitality, particularly for spiritual fathers who would benefit from immersion in family life and a place to kick back, rest awhile, and be fed good food. When my husband and I married, we made a point of this. One priest friend in particular has enjoyed the respite of our home, and we have been blessed by the gift of his presence and wisdom. It's important to remember that priests are called to be "in persona Christi," and Christ was a rabbi—a teacher.

The conversations we have had with our dear priest friend edify us every time and always involve learning from this wise teacher. One evening my husband and I had him over along with a newly married couple who were in the process of converting from Protestantism to Catholicism. As Father engaged us in conversation, he so naturally imparted teachings and life lessons. I felt like Mary at the feet of Jesus when she and her sister Martha hosted him at their home, or the disciples who encountered Jesus after the Resurrection on the road to Emmaus who said, "Were not our hearts burning within us while he was talking to us on the road, while he was opening the scriptures to us?" (Luke 24:32) Through connection, communion, and fellowship, I have personally experienced my intellectual life being fostered. Creating a home of hospitality where food and friendship come together facilitates this with ease.

In many ways, developing the intellect comes naturally because it is in our nature to learn; however, on various occasions we may find ourselves prone to pitfalls. Although my phone can lead me to content that expands my mind, it can also be a source of distraction when I find it more attractive to quickly scan headlines than to dive deep into materials of substance. As my husband has pointed out when referencing the importance of books, "What we pay attention to should have a spine." Granted, sometimes nuggets of wisdom can be communicated concisely, and not everything needs to be book length, but the point is that we mustn't neglect the pursuit of substance. That can be challenging when certain seasons of life are more exhausting than others.

During my first trimester of pregnancy, I felt so sick that the thought of reading or doing much of anything overwhelmed me. Exhaustion after birth also made me feel disinclined to read or to focus on intellectual pursuits. But life is full of seasons; it ebbs and flows. In seasons when we feel "dry," we can still pray and listen to others about what they are learning. When we are re-invigorated to be more intentional about learning again, we will feel the excitement and energy that comes from the contrast of no longer "taking a break." Prioritizing the sacraments and asking for God's grace to become who we are meant to be will also help us in our intellectual and spiritual maturation.

It is important to remember that our intellect is a gift, and with that comes a responsibility to foster its growth. As the Gospel of Matthew reminds us in the parable of the talents, when we are given something good we ought to cultivate it so it multiplies, not bury it and leave it to depreciation. Such growth and development is not just for ourselves but for sharing with others. Our learning should always be a complement to maintaining a communion of persons. This way, the God-given gift of our intellect becomes a gift we share and bless others with.

Benedictine Spirituality and the Mysteries of God

Elizabeth Scalia

Often my husband and I have remarked that one of the great privileges of our married life together was being able to survive on one paycheck when our children were infants and little ones. Financially, it was more than challenging; many were the months when we dug into couch cushions and rolled loose change in order to scrape together the price of a haircut for him, and things like eating out and going to the movies—those all fell by the wayside, at least for the first seven or eight years.

It wasn't easy. But it was worth it. In hindsight, the memories of enjoying long walks on brilliant autumn days, of picnicking in an old graveyard, or of discovering new parks to read and run in under shady trees are the dominant ones—the sweet ones I find myself lingering over as I embrace my crone-age. I walk the familiar old graveyards, all alone except for the chattering crows, and the ghosts of those years are revived as my gaze wanders the familiar rows—a glimpse of one son making a rubbing of a beautifully carved, fading headstone; an echo of the other, laughing as he falls from the branch he'd been climbing.

These are warm, lovely recollections, the sorts of reminiscences I expect to draw close to me as I approach my culmination, revisiting every part of my life as I fade away.

But they are bittersweet memories, too, because while so much about that time was precious, the early years of my motherhood did sometimes include a heavy sense of intellectual boredom that would weigh me down. As the first of our friends to have kids, all of my contemporaries were still employed and other-directed; my husband, trying to keep us afloat, worked two jobs. I wasn't lonely, exactly—I've been a rather solitary person all my life, with books and responsibilities keeping any sense of isolation at bay—but some days would find me longing for adult conversation, for the rich mental stimulation that comes from exchanging ideas with another—mind on mind kindling warmth. My sons were both bright (and children often have a way of offering up confoundingly true observations that can stop us in our tracks), but even the brightest three- or four-year-old is a less-than-satisfactory interlocutor when one wants to volley back and forth about the headlines. "You don't get it," I would sometimes kvetch to my exhausted husband. "You may be busy at work, but you still get to have adult conversation as you're plowing through the day or eating lunch. I spent my lunch today eating peanut butter and listening to your son and his preschool friend repeating 'poopyhead' to each other and then collapsing into giggles. Over and over again. For what felt like a *very* long time."

Consuming news and news byproducts—op-eds and the analysis of "experts" on social issues, the economy, and politics—kept my synapses firing. I would find myself developing arguments against a provocative opinion piece as I cleaned the bathroom, making such an energetic, passionate counterpoint to the air that my scrubbing would become downright prodigious. Sometimes, physically trapped by a napping child sprawled over my lap, I would turn a magazine page and read pundits whose voices I might normally ignore and discover that I liked reading an essay by John Leo as much as I liked reading articles by Calvin Trillin, or Hunter S. Thompson, or Florence King, or Christopher Hitchens, or Hannah Arendt. Without design, I developed a habit of reading disparate voices, and that helped me feel like I was intellectually branching out, or at least broadening my exposure to other perspectives, which I would process as I cleaned. Housework helped that along; when I turned off the radio and permitted my mind to wander while washing the floor or cleaning the fridge, I could simply let my own reason out to romp amid the well-articulated ideas I'd absorbed and see where it led me. Quite often, my own conclusions would surprise me. More than once, I found that—while I was not particularly "churchy" at that time—I had pondered my way into and out of a question only to splash-land with a surprise into Catholic orthodoxy.

Except, of course, when I didn't. Sometimes I would find myself moving past orthodoxy and into the ambiguities of Scripture—all those tantalizing verses that could mean more than one thing. "With God, nothing is impossible," for instance, could read as a straightforward testimony to the omnipotence of the Creator. But it could also mean that with God "nothing" is impossible—both a lesson in the delicious and infinite world of unimagined possibilities and surprising outcomes and a warning that to step away from God is to tempt a dance with the dark nothing where God is not.

Again, matters of faith were not hugely important to me at that time of my life, but (as is true with most of us who have been raised Catholic) the Gospels, the parables, and various lines from the epistles and the Old Testament were more deeply ingrained in me than I had ever realized, and my familiarity with those passages would seem to take me even beyond what I knew of the Catechism and into something like Holy Mystery—the vagaries of love brought deeply inside, inviting contemplation without my even really knowing what that meant from a Christian perspective.

One day, thanks to stumbling into Adoration and an unexpected encounter with the Holy Eucharist, Christ Jesus became important to me again—central to my life—and the Christian perspective seemed to inform everything. In previous years I had often jump-started an intellectual question by perusing one of the many historical anthologies or collections of quotations I'd amassed over the years—*Bartlett's Familiar Quotations* was always good for that—and now I was discovering biographies of saints and collections of their writings and diving into them. My world—which by then included baseball fields and band halls—continued to expand as I waited out my sons' rehearsals and activities in the company of G.K. Chesterton, C.S. Lewis, Augustine, Teresa of Avila, Graham Greene, Evelyn Waugh, and others.

But it was a modern poet and author—and a Presbyterian, to boot—who really charged and changed what I thought of as my intellectual life up to that point, and she did it with one cover-to-cover read of her 1996 bestseller *The Cloister Walk*. I'd picked up Kathleen Norris' book with absolutely no expectations (I hadn't even read a review of it) and found within its pages an invitation to look more closely at the Psalms, to investigate the Liturgy of the Hours—that age-old prayer of the Church that layfolk had long understood to be the sole province of clerics and religious—and ultimately to identify and dive into Benedictine spirituality, where I found the best and deepest expression of my own intellectual instincts and prayerful longings.

Having already discovered how remarkably ordinary work in the house and garden could help free the mind, permitting reason, imagination, and logic to flower seamlessly into contemplation, I found the Benedictine motto of *ora et labora* completely recognizable not simply as a mode of discipline but as a description of how our work feeds our prayer and our prayer ultimately instructs our work, especially when we realize—and it's a very Benedictine understanding—that we have no work of our own, that whatever task is before us is, ultimately, God's work, God's assignment, God's will placed before us.

It's one of those Benedictine things that, like the "conversion of manners" (choosing silence over adding to the din; self-effacement over self-promotion; having less instead of more), can paradoxically make you feel both less in step with "the world" and profoundly grounded within it.

As a lifelong (almost chronic) diarist who has always been more articulate through my pen than my tongue, the concept and practice of *lectio divina*, as laid out in monastic tradition and the *Holy Rule* of St. Benedict, simply brought definition and discipline to what I had already been doing for years and years—finding lines in my reading, or moments of striking insight pulled through a random quotation found here or there, and then expounding upon the line or the thought until I was either satisfied with my exploration of an idea or my hand grew tired.

But *lectio* was different, too, because it brought a sense of prayerful attention and intention to my journaling that had not been there before. "Listen carefully, my son, to the master's instructions," begins the prologue to the *Rule*, "and attend to them with the ear of your heart."[1] The words came at me like a siren call, at once familiar and encouraging: this "prayerful reading" of *lectio* meant slowing down, not plowing through a paragraph or treatise or line of Scripture but reading with something opened inside—with the "ear of the heart" awakened enough to perceive the nudging of the Holy Spirit calling me to particular attention, to something that, within the reading, is meant especially for me (for you!), for personal understanding, for increased spiritual and human growth. With *lectio*, journaling became a mode of prayer wherein I seemed to discern a heavenly outreach and was able to grab on to it, read, pray, and process it all in the moment, when my focus was most refined, and permit my own thoughts, my own lived-experience, my own gut to really "hear" the words and draw lessons and insights from them that might otherwise have escaped into the ether as I read.

The Cloister Walk became my Christmas and birthday gift to everyone I knew that year, but it also became the portal by which I entered into the rest of my life—one in which my intellect and my spirituality have over time become startlingly conjoined. I discerned a desire, and ultimately a call, to further embrace the Benedictine way as an Oblate. Taking on that charge has meant relearning my own way, sometimes over and over, for these past twenty years. It's meant volunteering at hospitals as a pastoral care visitor, learning (and ever-learning) how to be hospitable and a social host to others (receive everyone as Christ, says the *Rule*[2]) when my first and worst instinct is to want everyone to go away. It's meant making room each day for prayer and study, even when I don't especially feel like it. I may approach the oratory in my office with a sense of grumpy resignation sometimes, but the Liturgy of the Hours—and the always-instructive wellspring of the Psalms—will

---

1. Benedict, *The Rule*, in *St. Benedict Collection*, ed. Brandon Vogt (Park Ridge, IL: Word on Fire Classics, 2018), 7.
2. Benedict, *Rule*, 80.

reliably set me right, slow down my thoughts, my breath, my heartbeat, and invite me to renewed contemplation, even of ideas I had believed I'd already worked through.

The Liturgy of the Hours helps us to sanctify time; the Psalms teach us that there is truly nothing new under the sun—that twenty-first-century men and women carry within their hearts the same fears, joys, doubts, and violence as humanity ever has. The familiar lines and rhythms teach us that even our "settled thoughts" can rear up and bring a new question, surprising us with a new insight, and so it's okay—in fact, it might be the beginning of wisdom—to re-examine everything we think we know day by day with a willing, open "ear of the heart."

My embrace of Benedictine spirituality and the Psalms made me realize I could revisit any thought, ponder any one singular mystery—the Incarnation, for instance—every day for the rest of my life and never come to the end of all its wonders and quiet instruction. O pursuit of delight! I have become grateful for all of the mysteries—all of the ways I alternately learn more and more about God and love while still understanding so little—because they have helped me to learn patience with the great and unending mystery of the self.

The Vocation to Transformation

Amanda Achtman

As a young woman in my early twenties, I discovered that there is such a thing as the crisis of a lack of crisis, and that this is what I had. After having finished my undergraduate studies and worked for a couple of years, I was concerned that I was becoming too comfortable. What was my life actually about? Was I going to be doing the same thing forever? I had meaningful work that I enjoyed, lived in a city that was exciting, and had a circle of friends on whom I could rely. It became a paradox, then, that my being settled in this way actually began to unsettle me, making me restless.

Around this time, George Weigel, a biographer of John Paul II, came to Toronto to deliver a lecture. He spoke about the pope's dramatic life and legacy. After a sweeping overview, he concluded with the insight, "The noble life is still the most compelling witness for the fundamental truths that are the basis of our common world." These words gripped me. It was not merely what he said but the manner in which he said it: as someone who I could tell had been formed and transformed by its reality. At that moment, I knew that I wanted to become a student of noble lives.

I left my job, my country, and my comfort zone. I left for a new master's program that had just been launched in John Paul II Studies at the Catholic University of Lublin in Poland, where Karol Wojtyła had taught ethics before becoming pope. At the time, I knew very little about Poland. Yet, with the little information I had, I sensed that it was a country of saints, heroes, and martyrs that had something to teach me about how to live a life of greater meaning and depth.

Between the first and second year of my studies, I encountered George Weigel again—this time in the context of the Tertio Millennio Seminar on the Free Society. It was the twenty-fifth anniversary of this three-week program, which was founded to bring together young people from North America and Central and Eastern Europe to explore Catholic social teaching. Together, in a convivial atmosphere with excellent meals, beautiful liturgies, and inspiring excursions throughout Poland, we would immerse ourselves in authentic Catholic culture.

After checking into the accommodations at the student house of the Vincentian seminary, we gathered in an eleventh-century church at the foot of the Wawel Castle for an opening mass. A Polish Dominican, Fr. Maciej Zięba, spoke to us about the dramatic transformation in the lives of the Apostle Peter and in his 264th successor, Pope John Paul II.

What made young Simon, coming from peripheral and provincial Galilee, develop into the mature Peter leading the Church in Rome, the capital of the great empire? What led a twenty-year-old actor, risking his life during the German occupation for reciting Polish romantic poetry, to become a philosopher of human dignity and the defender of human rights all around the world? The answer for both, Fr. Zięba told us, was the close presence of Jesus, the transformative power of Christ's love.

Among the seminar participants were religious sisters, seminarians, newlyweds, young parents, lay people, politicians, new converts, journalists, economists, and artists from a dozen different countries. Fr. Zięba, who had been a friend of the pope and who spoke with wonder and credibility, captured our attention. Here he was giving us the key to how to become the fullness of who we could be—by letting ourselves be transformed by Christ. The next twenty days would be a highly experiential exploration of what this meant.

During a walking tour through Kraków, George Weigel said to us, "Try to be mindful that these streets through which we walk are the same ones a twenty-something-year-old man, who had no idea he would become a priest, much less change the history of the twentieth century, also walked. We are all called to be saints to fulfill our human and Christian destiny, and saints were people like us."

When I explored the streets of Kraków and heard dramatic stories of life interrupted by war, illness, family separation, loss, and grief, it was as though I was not so much speculating about what I might do next but rather learning the spiritual maturity to be able to contend with things not always going according to plan. Encountering historical friends from the difficult past century taught me concretely that their sanctity was forged through trials and that there is no Christian life without the cross. It is of course impossible to add yet-unknown crosses to our future plans, but we know that they will surely come, and so how do we prepare to bear them? Such questions chiseled our spiritual imagination.

On another day, after visiting the Jasna Góra Monastery at Częstochowa, we took a short drive to the St. Anna Convent, where we were served a typical Polish lunch by several cloistered Dominican nuns. Through a small revolving door, the food came out and volunteers from among our group brought the food to our tables. After our meal, we had an opportunity to visit the contemplative nuns through the grille. It was startling to encounter these women beaming from within their enclosure, and I felt as if God was saying to me, *Let yourself face up to these signs of contradiction against the conventions of your society that I am giving you.*

During the visit, a participant from our group asked what we could learn from their contemplative lives that we can apply to our Christian lives in the world. One sister answered in three parts: 1) First, silence. Silence is crucial not only for prayer but in order to develop a sense of integration as a human person. 2) The Rosary. The Rosary is simple and deep. It can be prayed while waiting for the bus or among many other daily activities. 3) Meditation on the Word of God.

After this point, Sr. Dominica added, "You can learn from our life, from our experience, that you can survive even in the most difficult circumstances. For example, I have been enclosed for forty years, and I am fine."

Another sister remarked, "We are enclosed and you are free; there is something to that. But spiritually, very often, we are free and you are the ones who are entangled. For me, freedom is life. And freedom poses the same question for us as it does for you. What should I do with it? What are my responsibilities? Whatever I do is a question of both freedom and responsibility. I consider myself free for God."

These were lives that, like works of art, make an impression. They summon from you the best you have to give, which is almost always more generous and audacious than you thought possible.

Later on, following some sessions on the principles of Catholic social teaching, we walked to the residence of the Archbishop of Kraków to visit Cardinal Stanisław Dziwisz. He had been very close to John Paul II, having served as his assistant and principal private secretary for forty years. We entered a room and took our seats, gazing up at a magnificent painting of John Paul II kneeling in prayer with a rosary in his hands and an ardent look on his face.

When Cardinal Dziwisz entered the room, we all rose to greet him. He said a few words that one of the Polish participants, Wojtek, translated into English for us:

John Paul II speaks not only through his legacy but also through his personality. Why do young people who never met or knew him still follow him? Because he was a witness of the things that are most beautiful. Now we remember him as a saint, so his legacy is also important. Let's remember his personality too. When people ask me where I saw his sanctity most clearly, it was most apparent in that he was a man of prayer. Then I am sometimes asked how many hours he prayed each day. Actually, his whole life was a prayer. Because he was so intensely united to God, everything he lived was a prayer. He said that his most important work as pope was prayer. So it is worth looking at closely!

As we were learning that the pope's results were born out of his relationship with God, one participant asked about the issues John Paul II urges us to take up in simple, practical ways in our everyday lives. "There are many issues," Cardinal Dziwisz began. "Respect for marriage, life, and the family. He laid out everything for us; we just have to look closely. Suffering was very present in his life. He kept saying that suffering has a sense, and, throughout his own life, he showed that suffering has a meaning and that our struggles can be transformed into something good."

In addition to contemplating suffering, we were also urged throughout the seminar to think about our death as a matter of ordinary Christian preparation. At a cemetery we visited in Zakopane, we paused at various graves and contemplated them, turning our attention away from Twitter bios and instead to epitaphs. As when I had first visited the churches in Rome, I was struck by the irony of materialists. We might expect materialists who think that this world is all there is and this life is all we have to create the most beautiful worldly things and to have the most elaborate graves for bodies. But they don't. Christians create the most beautiful churches and the most beautiful cemeteries. Our openness to transcendence and our faith in immortality enables the world to become so beautifully rich in symbolism and so filled with signs pointing beyond the objects themselves. The longing for the infinite and immaterial stirs us to create the most beautiful objects in the world—and to lead beautiful lives too.

As young people, it is easy to posture ourselves toward the next stage of our lives. Much of what we do at this age is in order to be able to do the next thing. There can also be a lot of pressure to account for ourselves and a sense of needing to justify our existence by our ambition or even by worthy aspirations. However, we never know how long we have, and so it helps now and again to step back and ask ourselves whether we are already doing the things that count. The world needs our witness to what really counts, that we are living out the adventure of our lives each and every day through him, with him, and in him.

By having a wide range of experiences, we see that the Christian life is not reducible but has many expressions. It is refreshing to discover that I do not define my own concept of existence and meaning, and thank God for that. What makes life meaningful is that we are not our own but rather belong to God, who loved us into existence. We also live in continuity with a great tradition, and we belong to one another and are a gift for each other. The feast days we celebrate, the prayers we pray together, and the liturgies that put us in communion with the saints bring all of this home.

Being available to study a panorama of sanctity gives inspiration and zeal for the day-to-day ways we are called to serve others. Throughout the world, there are many conferences, programs, seminars, retreats, and reading groups to which you can go to nourish your intellect in any season of life. This matters because it gives you an opportunity to see the breadth of the life of the Church, to discover what is possible, and to appreciate that the Christian life is not restricted to select fields, professions, or states in life but can be and is lived out in any and every circumstance.

The world needs goodness, beauty, and truth, and our tradition has it. We are called to actively receive these treasures ourselves in order to be able to share them with other hungry souls. Convivial Christian life consists of sharing experiences of meals, liturgies, books, art, music, and service. These are accessible to all of us if only we cultivate the taste for them such that we are not inclined to give them up. These experiences can be the occasion to find friends who "shine like stars in the world" (Phil. 2:15) and to learn to live your way into a more confident interiority without anguish and without conceits about the future.

Transformation in Christ depends upon moments of confrontation, turning points, and moments of decision. The greatness of these events is often hidden in our souls. Finally, it is worth mentioning that vocation is something better grasped in retrospect. As St. Edith Stein expresses so well:

This is how it was with the persons and events intertwined in the mystery of the Incarnation. Mary and Joseph, Zechariah and Elizabeth, the shepherds and the kings, Simeon and Anna—all of these had behind them a solitary life with God and were prepared for their special tasks before they found themselves together in those awesome encounters and events and, in retrospect, could understand how the paths left behind led to this climax.[1]

For us Catholics, faith is not only a matter of assent but of activity. We will have moments of difficulty, but we can never disregard the moments of true light. We do not unlearn insights or lose the kindnesses we have received. This, I think, is the confirmation of a personal vocation—that all through our lives, in great freedom and with great responsibility, we ate and drank with him (Acts 10:41); we lived our lives in the sight of God.

1. Edith Stein, *The Hidden Life: Hagiographic Essays, Meditations, Spiritual Texts*, ed. L. Gelber and Michael Linssen, trans. Waltraut Stein (Washington, DC: ICS Publications, 2014), 110.

The Joy of Thinking

Emily Stimpson Chapman

I was an unusual child. I said my first words at six months, took my first steps at eight months, and was reading by the time I turned three years old. I had no idea that was anything other than normal, and my parents had the good sense to never let me in on the secret. Instead, they happily fed my voracious appetite for books, never limiting me or insisting that I read at my age level. Accordingly, I read the Little House series at age five, the Chronicles of Narnia at age six, and *Anne of Green Gables* at age seven, the summer before second grade.

Back then, when I was deep in a book, it went with me wherever I went. Whatever I was reading was my companion, my best friend, my world. I disappeared into those books, tuning out everyone and everything around me as I raced from adventure to adventure with characters who were as real to me as my parents and sisters. Nothing but love motivated my reading. It was an experience of what St. Thomas Aquinas would call natural joy, a delight of the soul in encountering what is good.[1]

Not long after beginning second grade, however, I began to realize that my mind worked a little differently than my classmates'—more quickly, I guess. I pulled my head out of my books long enough to notice that my teacher gave me different work than she gave my classmates and that other adults seemed unusually focused on my vocabulary and my interest in

---

1. Thomas Aquinas, *Summa theologiae* 1-2.31.

things seven-year-olds aren't always interested in, such as the politics of the American Civil War.

I also started to enjoy the attention that came with that focus. I liked the praise. I liked the applause. I liked the gold stars on my classroom charts and the "Es" for "Exceeds Expectations" that covered the report cards I took home each quarter to my parents. I liked all of that so much that my desire for praise slowly overtook delight as my primary motivation for reading.

As the years passed, academic success became the lens through which I saw myself. It was, I thought, what defined me. And so I pursued it as an end in itself, wanting good grades, honors, and awards more than I wanted knowledge. I still enjoyed reading. I preferred it to lots of other things, like playing sports. But the joy I'd once found in diving deep into others' worlds and stories had dimmed.

It stayed dim straight through college, where I picked up majors like other young women picked up boys at bars, starting first with political science, then adding history, and after that English. I would jokingly tell people I had intellectual ADD—no subject could hold my attention for long. But, in a way, it was true. The only thing that seemed to hold my attention was keeping the highest grade point average in my university class, winning a host of academic awards, and getting the praise I craved from professors.

I *liked* what I studied. But I *loved* the praise that came from how well I studied. And the joy in discovering new worlds, ideas, and friends in books was all but gone. It had been driven out of my head and heart by more utilitarian concerns—scholarship money, prize money, job offers. That joy had also been driven out by my own insecurities—my need to feel like I had value, like I mattered. And where I found that value was in academic success.

That joy remained absent as I went to work on Capitol Hill and began graduate school in political theory at Johns Hopkins University. I didn't really want to study political theory, but the program was impressive and the degree practical, and it just seemed like the thing to do. Until I couldn't. A year into the program, I was bored out of my mind. I was still making straight As, but they weren't motivation enough anymore. They didn't last.

There was always another A to get, another professor to impress. There was no resting, no end to chasing applause and accolades. Success did not satisfy.

So, I did something I'd never done in my entire life: I quit. I dropped out of the program and walked away from being the star student, on track for a PhD, and became just another twenty-something working on Capitol Hill with no idea what she wanted to do with her life.

A New Vision

That's what I was doing in the summer of 2000 when a new guy came to work in our office. He was intelligent but a bit odd. He went to Mass on days besides Sunday. He talked about things like going to confession and praying the Rosary. And he seemed to take seriously what bishops and popes said. Even though I'd grown up Catholic, I'd never met anyone like that before. I thought that sort of thinking and believing had gone out of style after the Second Vatican Council.

To make matters even more confusing, he seemed to really love Jesus. He also knew his Bible way better than my Protestant friends did. I had no idea what to make of him.

Years earlier, I had left the Catholic Church, not really knowing what I was leaving. In college, I had met a cute, smart Protestant boy who helped me to think through questions of faith seriously for the first time. With his encouragement, I began a serious walk with Jesus. But I thought that walk had to lead me away from the Catholic Church. Now, here was this Rosary-praying, Bible-believing, Jesus-loving, Eucharist-receiving guy, blowing up all the boxes with which I approached questions of faith.

Obviously, I had to show him the error of his ways.

For months, we argued back and forth about the Church's hierarchy, the Eucharist, contraception, and every other issue that divided us. No matter how much I thought I knew, though, he always seemed to know more. And it drove me bonkers.

Then, one day, he offered me a book to read: *The Poet and the Lunatics* by G.K. Chesterton. I had no idea who Chesterton was, but the book was fictional, not obviously about Catholicism, so I took it. I'm still not sure why. I wasn't reading much of anything at the time. Reading had become so much about school, grades, and preparing papers that when I dropped out of my grad program, I dropped the last vestiges of my childhood reading habit as well.

But I did take the book. Then, a few days later, I flew home to Illinois for a weekend and brought the book to keep me company on the flight. What good company it was. With no paper to write about the book, no test to take on it, and no one to impress by reading it, I forgot more and more about myself with each turn of the page. Yet, by the time I closed that book, I had found myself—the reader, who approached every story with wonder and who rejoiced at encountering new people, ideas, and worlds through the yellowed pages of old books. I loved this Chesterton. I needed more!

My co-worker was happy enough to oblige. He brought in a stack of Chesterton books, and I began plowing through them just like my seven-year-old self had once plowed through *Anne of Green Gables*. Eventually, I came to *Orthodoxy*, Chesterton's great reflection on Christian tradition. All my defenses were down, and grace rushed in. Within two weeks, I had gone back to confession and was attending daily Mass at the parish across from my office. I was a practicing Catholic once more.

I needed more books, though. There was so much I didn't know. There was so much I wanted to know. So, my co-worker kept the books coming: *Theology and Sanity* by Frank Sheed, *The Spirit of Catholicism* by Karl Adam, *Chance or the Dance?* by Thomas Howard, *The Intellectual Life* by A.G. Sertillanges, and book after book by Peter Kreeft, Dietrich von Hildebrand, Christopher Dawson, John Paul II, and so many more. I read them all as fast as I could—in the morning between teaching fitness classes and starting my workday; in the evening after work, at my favorite coffee shop; on Saturdays, all day after morning Mass; and on every lunch break I had.

I couldn't get enough—of reading, of learning, of discovering who God was and who I was and why the world was the way it was. It was all a delight.

It was all joy. And not just the natural joy of losing myself in a good book, but the supernatural joy that is a fruit of the Holy Spirit, an encounter with Christ that helps us to see goodness, beauty, and hope even in the midst of sorrow.

The more I read about the faith, the more my vision of the world was changed. And the more my vision was changed, the more joy I rediscovered in reading—not just theology books, but fiction, poetry, cultural commentary, all of it. Because, at last, I had found the thread that connected all the stories I'd ever loved, all the stories ever told. It was the faith. It was reality. It was seeing the world and all that was in it as God wanted me to see it. That seeing was a joy, and that seeing led to greater joy. It led me to Christ, the source of our joy. And it led me to wisdom, which guided me as I strove to live, work, and love in a way that was rooted in truth, which is to say, in a way that was rooted in Christ.

Lessons Learned

It's been twenty years now since I found my joy in reading again—or, more specifically, in reading both about the faith and with the eyes of faith. And I haven't lost that joy yet. I haven't grown bored or tired of reading about Catholicism, writing about Catholicism, or thinking about Catholicism. I don't know how one could. Catholicism, as my husband says, is like honey; it gets all over everything. It gets all over history and friendship, sex and suffering, motherhood and marriage, food and fashion, literature and politics, even home design. It touches everything, illuminates everything, transforms everything.

It's more than that, though. I didn't just find my joy in reading again because I was reading the right material. I found it because I was reading for the right *reason*. I wasn't pursuing a career. I wasn't seeking a certain grade. I wasn't doing what my parents, professors, or bosses wanted me to do. I was reading because I wanted to read. I was reading because I wanted to learn more and understand more. I wanted knowledge. I wanted wisdom. I wanted to expand my vision of the beautiful, broken world God had made and see every last atom of it as he sees it.

I also was lucky enough to be doing that way back at the beginning of the millennium, before the advent of iPhones, social media, and watches that are smarter than all of us. I could give myself completely to what I was learning without constant distraction. I could sit in a world that was less noisy, less busy, and let the words on the page, instead of the words on the internet, fill my soul.

There may be many secrets to finding joy in the intellectual life and finding the specific branch of knowledge whose pursuit brings you the most joy, but these are the three I know. And this is how you can put them to use in your own search.

First, don't try to seek knowledge apart from faith; seek knowledge with the eyes of faith, remembering, as A.G. Sertillanges wrote, "Everything holds treasures. . . . Every road opened is a corridor to God."[2]

Second, don't set out on this path for anyone but you and God. Don't study something because it's what your parents want you to study. Don't pursue a career to gain applause or approval. Don't chase being the best simply to be the best. Read what brings you pleasure. Study what captures your imagination. Dive deeper and deeper into what holds your attention and gives you life. It's there, following the way of your interests and abilities, that you will find the path to which God calls you.

Finally, focus. Give whatever you are reading, writing, or thinking about your full attention. Put the phone down. Take your headphones out. Leave the watch in another room. Make space in your head or heart for knowledge to plant itself there and start bearing fruit.

One last thing to remember: in *The Great Divorce*, C.S. Lewis' fictional journey through the afterlife, his guide, George MacDonald, promises him, "No soul that seriously and constantly desires joy will ever miss it. Those who seek find. To those who knock it is opened."[3]

---

2. A.G. Sertillanges, *The Intellectual Life: Its Spirit, Conditions, Methods*, trans. Mary Ryan (Washington, DC: The Catholic University of America Press, 1998), 73.
3. C.S. Lewis, *The Great Divorce* (New York: HarperOne, 2001), 75.

That's true of finding joy in the life of the mind as well.

Keep your eyes on Christ, study what you love for its own sake, and give the work at hand your full attention. Do all that, and you won't have to look for joy in the intellectual life. It will find you.

The School of Leisure

Jennifer Frey

Americans tend to place supreme value on hard work, usefulness, and productivity. While we look forward to a nice retirement, we tend to think of this as a reward for the more meaningful life of work that preceded it. Consequently, we tend to think of our leisure time as a period of relaxation and respite—necessary periods of "self-care" so that we can return to the serious business of work. Nor is this mentality confined to the breadwinner of the family; stay-at-home mothers can also define the value of their lives in terms of purposeful domestic work, which never seems to end. This workism, in any context, takes work as the most valuable mode of existence and thinks of the importance of leisure in relation to it.

But the Church cautions against workism. In his letter addressed to women, Pope St. John Paul II writes that one of "the serious problems of the future" is the need for "leisure time" (*tempo libero*) and that he thinks women can help to reclaim it. He writes:

> A greater presence of women in society will prove most valuable, for it will help to manifest the contradictions present when society is organized solely according to the criteria of efficiency and productivity, and it will force systems to be redesigned in a way which favors the processes of humanization which mark the "civilization of love."[1]

1. Pope John Paul II, "Letter to Women" 4, June 29, 1995, vatican.va.

John Paul II further points us to Mary, the Mother of God, as the clearest and highest expression of the "feminine genius" that we need to draw upon in order to imagine a different, less work-focused world.

These are intriguing suggestions. To try to make sense of them, let us begin our reflections with a definition of work. When I speak about the difference between work and leisure, I am not picking out external conditions, such as whether you are on vacation or in the office, because you could spend your vacation in work mode and your office time in a state of inner leisure. The real difference between work and leisure is not primarily external but internal: it lies in our habits of mind and heart. When we are working, our minds are busy with the task at hand, and we operate in an instrumental mode of thinking, in which the goodness of what is done is defined as a *means* to some determinate, productive end. For example, we do laundry in order to have fresh clothing to wear, and we prepare food in order to feed our families. We judge work by its utility value; the work either produces the desired result and is good or does not and is bad.

Leisure (*tempo libero*) is the opposite of work and is an altogether different habit of being. In leisure, one's mind is receptive rather than active, and there is no need for great effort or exertion because there is no external purpose or goal that needs to be accomplished. And that is because leisure is a space of intrinsic value; in leisure, one *enjoys* or takes delight in what is intrinsically true, good, and beautiful: music, a sunset, the presence of a loved one, a good story, a poem, or perhaps one's own memories.

In the Catholic intellectual tradition, leisure is explicitly connected to contemplation, which can be defined as beholding, in vision, an object of love. The Church recognizes the strong connection between love and attention and has long taught that the will directs our attention toward the objects it desires. Contemplation, then, is not a stance of neutral observation; rather, it requires proper habits of love, desire, feeling, imagination, perception, and judgment that are only developed in a space of leisure. The Catholic philosopher Josef Pieper writes:

> Leisure is a form of silence, of that silence which is the prerequisite of the apprehension of reality. . . . Silence, as it is used in this context, does not mean "dumbness" or "noiselessness"; it means more nearly that the soul's power to "answer" to the reality of the world is left undisturbed. For leisure is a receptive attitude of mind, a contemplative attitude, and it is not only the occasion but also the capacity for steeping oneself in the whole of creation.[2]

Leisure is not simply a description of one's environment, but rather a set of abilities that require silence and solitude. In silence, we draw ourselves away from the busy world that we are ordered to, realizing our intentions, and contemplate that which transcends it. In contemplative silence, we become less bent over the brooding self and more open to beauty, which naturally brings us outside the space where the demands of the selfish ego are loudest. The secular philosopher Iris Murdoch gives an example of such contemplative "unselfing":

> I am looking out of my window in an anxious and resentful state of mind, oblivious of my surroundings, brooding perhaps on some damage done to my prestige. Then suddenly I observe a hovering kestrel. In a moment everything is altered. The brooding self with its hurt vanity has disappeared. There is nothing now but kestrel. And when I return to thinking of the other matter it seems less important. And of course this is something which we may also do deliberately: give attention to nature in order to clear our minds of selfish care.[3]

Murdoch aligns herself with classical tradition in connecting virtue with contemplation of what is beautiful. The idea is that our knowledge of the good attracts us toward it and outside of ourselves; this attraction elicits in us a desire to become conformed to the good we see. Murdoch stresses that we

---

2. Josef Pieper, *Leisure: The Basis of Culture* (San Francisco: Ignatius Press, 2009), 46–47.
3. Iris Murdoch, *Existentialists and Mystics* (New York: Penguin, 1997), 369.

only come to appreciate the good when we are properly receptive to it, and this requires that we be able to pay attention. The cultivation of virtue is born first and foremost in contemplative leisure, when we learn to see, appreciate, and respond to what is true, good, and beautiful.

Catholic tradition teaches that our greatest example of the right use of leisure—of contemplation—is Mary, the Mother of God. Mary spent a life in earthly contemplation of the highest earthly object—the face of her son, Jesus Christ. Our traditions of sacred art are a testament to this contemplation; in how many paintings is Mary gazing lovingly or sorrowfully upon the face of her son? In his beautiful apostolic letter *Rosarium Virginis Mariae*, John Paul II teaches that Mary is an "incomparable model" of the contemplation of Christ. Of the necessity and value of such contemplation, he writes:

> To look upon the face of Christ, to recognize its mystery amid the daily events and the sufferings of his human life, and then to grasp the divine splendor definitively revealed in the Risen Lord, seated in glory at the right hand of the Father: this is the task of every follower of Christ and therefore the task of each one of us. In contemplating Christ's face we become open to receiving the mystery of Trinitarian life, experiencing ever anew the love of the Father and delighting in the joy of the Holy Spirit. Saint Paul's words can then be applied to us: "Beholding the glory of the Lord, we are being changed into his likeness, from one degree of glory to another; for this comes from the Lord who is the Spirit" (2 Cor. 3:18).[4]

Again, here we see that contemplative vision of the good has transformative potential on a spiritual level.

While John Paul II associates Mary with the contemplation of Christ in the flesh, there is a venerable artistic and theological tradition that draws on an ideal of Mary as a contemplative even prior to Christ's conception. In this tradition, when the angel Gabriel comes to announce that she has been chosen to give birth to the son of God, Mary is depicted as withdrawn from

---

4. Pope John Paul II, *Rosarium Virinis Mariae* 9, apostolic letter, October 16, 2002, vatican.va.

the world, deep in the silence and solitude of study.[5] This depiction has theological roots dating back to the early Church Fathers, who taught that Mary's study was the source of the rich inner life that enabled her to freely consent to the divine offer the angel conveyed to her. Catholic tradition has long recognized this tie between the quality of contemplation and the cultivation of true freedom—with Mary as the model.

I want to expand upon these Marian themes in order to argue that spending our leisure time in study is central to the life of women. As Aquinas defines study, quite broadly, it is a kind of focused attention on some object that is worthy of it.[6] One can study nature, art, a person, or a subject matter. Study as I use it here should not be understood as work but as leisure. Study for the sake of good grades, or a good career, or for the sake of the fulfillment of any of our ambitions is not contemplative study. Contemplative study is done for the sake of truth alone, which is the good of the intellect. Study is important to Aquinas, because he argues that our desire for the truth finds its ultimate fulfillment in the beatific vision; only then is the fullness of truth attained and this natural desire completely satisfied.

The French philosopher and mystic Simone Weil is helpful in understanding the spiritual fruits of study, since she explicitly links study with contemplation and prayer. Weil understands study as indispensable to the cultivation of the inner dispositions necessary to achieve true freedom and intimacy with God. Weil cautions that we should not study for any instrumental end. Rather, we should study simply to grow in the truth, because our happiness and ultimate end is, as Augustine and Aquinas both affirm, "joy in the truth."[7] Weil argues:

> Quite apart from explicit religious belief, every time that a human being
> succeeds in making an effort of attention with the sole idea of increasing

---

5. Zena Hitz, *Lost in Thought: The Hidden Pleasures of an Intellectual Life* (Princeton, NJ: Princeton University Press, 2020), 59–63.

6. Thomas Aquinas, *Summa theologiae* 1-2.166.1.

7. Augustine, *Confessions*, trans. F.J. Sheed, ed. Michael P. Foley (Park Ridge, IL: Word on Fire Classics, 2017), 255.

his grasp of truth, he acquires a greater aptitude for grasping it, even if his effort produces no visible fruit. . . . Even if our efforts of attention seem for years to be producing no result, one day a light which is in exact proportion to them will flood the soul. Every effort adds a little gold to a treasure which no power on earth can take away.[8]

Weil recognizes that our contemplative attention is a moral and spiritual capacity—it is ultimately the substance of our prayer life. In study, we develop the habits of attention that allow for a richer prayer life and intimacy with God. The first and most essential fruits of study, according to Weil, are in the interior life. Our study informs the way we see the world, allowing us to achieve a deeper, more penetrating vision of reality, and this in turn enables us to cultivate the dispositions that regulate our appetite to know and seek the truth. It is in the fulfillment of this desire for truth, which study sharpens, that our perfect happiness consists.

We are now, at last, in a position to diagnose the contradictions of workism. In a society that treats leisure as necessary for work, the highest goods in human life become marginalized, for these are the goods that demand leisure: friendship, family, knowledge, virtue, and divine worship. These goods are not measured in terms of their usefulness or how efficiently they produce measurable results. They belong to an altogether higher order, such that what is merely productive and efficient are for the sake of it.

Why does John Paul II suggest that women are uniquely positioned to reclaim the value of leisure? I believe that it is, in part, because women, as mothers, teachers, and caregivers, have a natural closeness and special bond to children, who are creatures for whom work is alien and leisure natural. When we are brought into the life of children, especially when we play with them and seek to educate them at an early age, we step outside the space of work and into a space of discovery, wonder, and celebration. The theologian Romano Guardini reminds us that the child is able to celebrate its existence through its play. He writes:

8. Simone Weil, *Waiting for God* (New York: HarperCollins, 2009), 59.

The child, when it plays, does not aim at anything. It has no purpose. It does not want to do anything but to exercise its youthful powers, pour forth its life in an aimless series of movements, words and actions, and by this to develop and to realize itself more fully; all of which is purposeless, but full of meaning nevertheless, the significance lying in the unchecked revelation of this youthful life in thoughts and words and movements and actions, in the capture and expression of its nature, and in the fact of its existence.[9]

Children are able to celebrate their existence as good in itself and to delight in it, and they are able to do this because they are free from the demands of work. Guardini goes on to compare child's play to divine worship. The liturgy has nothing to do with the world of human purpose and ambition; it is about God and directs all of our energies toward him. In liturgy, art and reality become united in "a supernatural childhood before God," teaching us how to be in leisure:

The soul must learn to abandon, at least in prayer, the restlessness of purposeful activity; it must learn to waste time for the sake of God, and to be prepared for the sacred game with sayings and thoughts and gestures, without always immediately asking "why?" and "wherefore?" It must learn not to be continually yearning to do something, to attack something, to accomplish something useful, but to play the divinely ordained game of the liturgy in liberty and beauty and holy joy before God.[10]

Divine worship is the highest expression of human leisure, and yet there is an element of play in it—it too is a celebration of existence itself.

In the life of children, there is also a close kinship between the affinity for play and a sense of wonder. In their unstructured playtime, children often indulge their natural appetite for truth. For them, in part because they are

---

9. Romano Guardini, *The Spirit of the Liturgy*, trans. Ada Lane (Edmond, OK: Veritatis Splendor Publications, 2012), 99.

10. Guardini, 93.

free from the demands of work and are allowed to be bored, their natural wonder is uninhibited. Children are easily amazed at what they discover—they delight in learning when they are allowed to be naturally inquisitive about what they encounter, when they are encouraged to marvel at the world they are exploring. It is this natural joy that must be harnessed when it comes time for more formal study, for without love and desire for truth, our study is fruitless. Aquinas teaches that the contemplative life—the life of study and prayer—is ultimately motivated by charity.[1] Just as it was love that drove the Virgin Mary to contemplate the face of her son, so we must teach our children to contemplate out of love—to connect the love of truth with its highest fulfillment. We must teach them that every truth sought "is the image of something precious" because every particular truth is "a pure image of the unique, eternal, and living Truth, the very Truth that one in a human voice declared: 'I am the Truth.'"[2]

It is sometimes suggested that women do not need to study beyond the practical arts because their main goal is to manage the household and to raise children. This is sometimes proclaimed by the very same people who hold Mary up as the ideal woman. And yet, tradition understands and reveres Mary not as a domestic manager but as a model of the contemplative life, a woman for whom study and contemplation are essential pursuits. If this is not the highest expression of her feminine genius, it is hard to fathom what is.

As mothers and as teachers, we must help our children to find joy in the truth; we must cultivate this natural desire so that it is ordered to our ultimate, highest end. This is the school of leisure, and even if we do not have children of our own, it is always incumbent upon us to make sure that this school of leisure does not get sacrificed to the totalizing ideology of workism.

Workism forgets that our highest goal and purpose is nothing more or less than rest in the divine life. If we spend our free time well, we spend it resting in the good, finding joy in the truth, celebrating existence itself. This earthly leisure is a foretaste of our perfect and eternal rest in God's glory that is our

---

1. Thomas Aquinas, *ST* 2-2.180.7.
2. Weil, *Waiting for God*, 62.

true calling and fulfillment. When we see God face to face, when we behold him with the eyes of our heart, we rest in an inexhaustible goodness, and this delight is the fulfillment of our deepest desire and longing, the perfect fruit of charity. There is, in the beatified life, no work. A true civilization of love will never lose sight of this.

Pursuit in the Drudgery

Leah Libresco Sargeant

Betty Friedan's *The Feminine Mystique* is a modern primer in acedia. Her interviews with frustrated housewives are written from a secular perspective, but they speak to the thwarted exhaustion that is the fruit of sloth. Sloth isn't a matter of inactivity but, as St. Thomas Aquinas puts it in the *Summa theologiae*, "sadness about one's spiritual good."[3]

Keeping a home and caring for others are good work for women and men to undertake, but the wives that Friedan interviews are suffocated by their roles and the thin support they receive. Friedan notes that what these women feel is something different than simple exhaustion—rest offers little relief. When the wives she speaks to have the opportunity for an hour to themselves, "they often gave it up on the slightest pretext, either from guilt or from boredom."[4]

Betty Friedan, to my knowledge, isn't cited explicitly in Robert Cardinal Sarah's *The Power of Silence: Against the Dictatorship of Noise*. But over fifty years after her work, formed by a rural childhood in Guinea and life serving the Church globally, Sarah observes the same discomfort with quiet and leisure. He writes:

> Without noise, man is feverish, lost. Noise gives him security . . . [it] is a whirlwind that avoids facing itself. Agitation becomes a tranquilizer, a

---

3. Thomas Aquinas, *Summa theologiae* 1-2.84.4.
4. Betty Friedan, *The Feminine Mystique* (New York: W.W. Norton, 2001), 471.

sedative, a morphine pump, a sort of reverie, an incoherent dream-world. But this noise is a dangerous, deceptive medicine, a diabolic lie that helps man avoid confronting himself in his interior emptiness.[5]

Time for yourself is little consolation if you don't have a sense of who your *self* is supposed to be. Busyness at least offers a distraction from that sense that something is rotten at the core of the life you live. As Friedan puts it, "A woman who has no purpose of her own in society, a woman who cannot let herself think about the future because she is doing nothing to give herself a real identity in it, will continue to feel a desperation in the present."[6]

Drudgery and desperation go together. The day can narrow to an endless cycle of tasks done and redone, with nothing ever feeling *completed*. The work of the home is repetitive—every meal means taking out the pans and dishes, working to prepare the meal, and then taking on the final task of making the work of the meal invisible again. Every dish washed, dried, and removed from view; every tool removed from the wiped-down counters; every leftover boxed and bagged and settled behind the doors of the fridge. Women's work frequently follows this pattern of effort and then additional labor to hide the evidence of effort.

As Friedan saw it, the only solution is to escape the cycle of dry drudgery. She writes, "The only way for a woman, as for a man, to find herself, to know herself as a person, is by creative work of her own. There is no other way."[7] Friedan is quick to say that there's no guarantee that a job *outside* the home will meet this criterion. Drudgery is not elevated by being performed in an office instead of a kitchen. She wants to see women enter work that is "equal to their actual capacity" and allows them to "develop the lifetime interests and goals which require serious education and training."

These kinds of work are part of a full and flourishing life. Friedan praises both women who take on paid jobs as well as those who find ways

---

5. Robert Cardinal Sarah, *The Power of Silence: Against the Dictatorship of Noise* (San Francisco: Ignatius Press, 2017), 33.

6. Friedan, *Feminine Mystique*, 471.

7. Friedan, 472.

to serve their communities as volunteers by founding mental health clinics or educational programs. The women do good for others while challenging themselves. But the question lingers: is the time spent not being challenged, the time spent in cleaning and cooking and maintenance, a time devoid of growth and life?

Cloistered religious live lives of repetition. Every day follows the same routine, with meals to cook and laundry to do and sisters to accompany in love and silence. Nothing obvious is amassed at the end of the day. Rosary beads pass through their fingers in a closed circle; nothing about the prayer shows outwardly how many *Aves* have been stacked up or how fervently they were felt. Work reaches its completion only in death—and the consummation is not visible to those left behind on earth.

So what can motivate the work that is never done, work that isn't as obviously spiritually elevated as time spent in Adoration? The most romantic call to arms for repetitive work that I've encountered comes from G.K. Chesterton in *Orthodoxy*. He isn't initially speaking of the labor of the home but of theories of politics, progress, and decline:

> We have remarked that one reason offered for being a progressive is that things naturally tend to grow better. But the only real reason for being a progressive is that things naturally tend to grow worse. . . . All conservatism is based upon the idea that if you leave things alone you leave them as they are. But you do not. If you leave a thing alone you leave it to a torrent of change. If you leave a white post alone it will soon be a black post. If you particularly want it to be white you must be always painting it again; that is, you must be always having a revolution. Briefly, if you want the old white post you must have a new white post. But this which is true even of inanimate things is in a quite special and terrible sense true of all human things. An almost unnatural vigilance is really required of the citizen because of the horrible rapidity with which human institutions grow old.[8]

---

8. G.K. Chesterton, *Orthodoxy* (Park Ridge, IL: Word on Fire Classics, 2017), 114–115.

Painting the fence post again and again is the work of sustaining national institutions, but it's also the work of sustaining a home, a relationship. When the work is *not* neglected, it's easy to feel like the daily maintenance is futile or unimportant. When the work is done well, it is unremarkable and often unremarked upon, making the labor feel lonely.

In my own house, my husband and I keep a little whiteboard on the fridge for chores and other daily acts of maintenance. The little checkmarks next to each of our own names make the work a little more visible to each other—and to ourselves. There's a satisfaction in seeing the check mark next to "wash sippy cups" that *proves* the work is done, even as the sippy cup looks the same from a distance or is secreted away somewhere mysterious by our toddler.

We have something of a model for pursuit in her. When we watch her climb up onto chairs that are *almost* too high for her, she isn't doing it to sit at leisure but to explore the edge of her mastery, to come to know and love her body. As Maria Montessori writes, "The child of this age sets out to do a certain task, perhaps an absurd one to adult reasoning, but this matters not at all; he must carry out the activity to its conclusion. There is a vital urge to completeness of action."[9]

In this, a child lives out the call to holiness and perfection through work suggested by St. Josemaría Escrivá and the Opus Dei movement he founded. In *Furrow*, he writes,

> Before God, no occupation is in itself great or small. Everything gains the value of the Love with which it is done.

> Heroism at work is to be found in finishing each task.

> Let me stress this point: it is in the simplicity of your ordinary work, in the monotonous details of each day, that you have to find the secret, which is hidden from so many, of something great and new: Love.[10]

9. Maria Montessori, *Education for a New World* (Santa Barbara, CA: Clio Press, 1989), 45.
10. Josemaría Escrivá, *Furrow* (New York: Scepter, 2002), 191.

It is easier for my daughter to find delight in the monotonous details and give her whole heart to them than it is for me. For her, most challenges are new—even when she has mastered a skill, in a few months her body has grown and changed and she must learn to approach it afresh to make best use of her new capacities.

I sometimes go through a similar renewal in my tasks, but it is usually the result of a *diminished* or a *diverted* capacity rather than an expanded one. How can I reach into the depths of the washing machine when my increasingly rounded belly holds me at a distance? When will my post-surgical pain be at its lowest ebb so I can take careful steps down the hospital corridor to aid my recovery? How can I sauté these onions one-handed while my baby sits on my hip and tries to cantilever herself toward the sputtering oil?

These challenges don't always feel welcome. And persisting *through* them, relying on my own strength, isn't always the right answer. Maria Montessori urges parents to nourish their child by setting appropriate work before them. "Fatigue also is caused by work unsuitable to the individual. Suitable work reduces fatigue on account of the pleasure derived from the work itself. Thus the two causes of fatigue are unsuitable work and premature interruption of work."[11] Both stumbling blocks are familiar to working women and mothers.

Everything set before us *can* be offered to God, but we are permitted to ask for help, from him or from our friends, so that we have the space to restore our right relation to work. There is nothing lost by turning some tasks over to automation or to others—I have no desire to wash my clothes by hand. The goal is to have a little space and silence to do at least some work single-mindedly.

Offering our exterior work to God can help form us to offer our interior life to him. The physical repetition of a Rosary or a daily cycle of prayers is meant to begin a work that is not abandoned when the beads are put away or the Angelus bells stop ringing. Our goal is to dwell with God at all times,

---

11. Maria Montessori, *What You Should Know About Your Child* (Chennai, India: Kalakshetra Publications, 1961), 135.

to "Rejoice always, pray without ceasing, give thanks in all circumstances," as St. Paul reminds us, "for this is the will of God in Christ Jesus for you" (1 Thess. 5:16–18).

The challenge is to rejoice without needing to have an accomplishment of our own to celebrate. When I meditate on the mysteries of the Rosary, I don't *discover* something new about God that I can excitedly reveal to him as proof of my devotion. I am simply present with him, receiving what he chooses to give.

Unremarkable work done out of love is our reminder that we don't have to secret ourselves away and amass accomplishments in order to win God's love. We are loved—we could not be conserved in existence without his loving attention. Offering our smallest work is our opportunity to practice holding nothing back from him.

If we can invite him into our dullest moments, our least exciting tasks, and our monotony, we will have fewer spaces where we feel abandoned by him or that we are tempted to hide from him. Our quiet, not-obviously-interesting work is practice in remembering that our whole lives are his. These small challenges prepare us to extend the harder invitation—asking God into our moments of weakness, shame, and sin.

Every moment of recollection in a moment that doesn't feel *worthy* of God is a pledge of faith that he is with us in every moment. There is no door too humble for him to open, no soul too small to catch up into his love, no work that is wasted if it is done in love for him and his people.

The Feminine Intellect and Academia

Holly Ordway

The other contributors to this book have had much to say about the way that women can, and should, develop the life of the mind in whatever state of life or vocation they have. One particular vocation that is (or at least seems) inseparably connected with the idea of the intellect is that of being in *academia*. I am myself an academic, and I love what I do.

One thing that I get to do is advise people who feel that they are called to a life in academia and want to know how to go about it. It's precisely because I care about mentoring young academics that I'm now going to throw several buckets full of icy cold water over the heads of women (and men too) who may be dreaming about a career in the academic world. Stick with me! It'll be bracing, but good for you.

All too often, academic life is romanticized and idealized, which means that young people often set themselves the ambition of being "in academia" without properly considering what that entails and what sort of work one might reasonably expect to do as an academic. As a result, if they do pursue such a career, they go about it with insufficient preparation and unrealistic expectations and end up disappointed, indebted, and depressed.

As an advisor of graduate students, many of whom would ask me about pursuing doctoral work immediately after finishing their master's degree under my supervision, I would (and still do) set before them all the reasons why it would be better for them *not* to get a PhD. If, after seriously taking into consideration all the difficulties and sacrifices ahead, they still felt drawn to the academic life, we would then have a conversation about how they might move forward.

What I wish to do here is to help you, the reader, remove any rose-colored glasses that you might unknowingly be wearing when you look at the academic life. For your own well-being and the sake of your future vocation, I wish to disabuse you of any romantic notions you may have. Only the independently wealthy can read, think, and study as ends in themselves. The rest of us have to earn a living, and doing so in academia is not glamorous; it's often exhausting, and it's usually not very exciting. In short, it's much like any other profession or vocation when viewed from the inside. It's good work (if you can get it—more on that in a moment!) but it's hard work.

What exactly is "academia"? The Oxford English Dictionary defines it as "the academic community; the world of university scholarship." An academic is generally considered to be "a member of a university or college's teaching or research staff" or, more generally, "a person interested in or excelling at pursuits involving reading, thinking, and study."

Here we can detect two ways of seeing academic life: on the one hand, being a university teacher or researcher, doing scholarship; on the other, being part of a community of people who care deeply about and strive for excellence in the life of the mind. The two are closely related and often (even usually) overlap, but they are not the same.

Let's consider the first view of being an academic: working as a university teacher or researcher. To be an academic of this kind is, fundamentally, to *teach*, to share knowledge and transmit wisdom. At the big research universities, sadly, this is too often sidelined in favor of getting grants and publishing papers, but fortunately there are still many smaller colleges that focus on teaching. And here's the first splash of cold water. Teaching is not characterized by sitting around having deep discussions with young people eager to benefit from your insights. Rather, it's best understood as the quotidian reality of papers to grade, syllabi to update according to the latest convoluted regulations from the administration, more papers to grade, committee meetings to attend, still more papers to grade, reports to file, and, above all, the fact that many of your students will be academically underprepared, anxious, and overwhelmed. Furthermore, you'll rarely get to teach advanced classes in your special subject; instead, you'll mostly teach basic undergraduate courses.

Being a good academic means being willing to roll up your sleeves and meet your students where they are, not where you wish they were or feel they ought to be. This is difficult and often discouraging work, frequently made more burdensome by endlessly multiplying bureaucratic reporting requirements. (Say "outcomes and assessment" to a full-time professor and see how they shiver!) The work is vitally important and can be deeply satisfying, but its rewards are subtle, and teachers seldom receive outward recognition.

When academics, as a professional class, are not teaching, we are usually writing. This, too, is hard work, and what's more, much of it we do without getting paid. Academics almost never earn money from writing articles for academic journals or contributing chapters to academic books; we do it for the advancement of the field in general and for the development of our careers in particular. If we can, we also write books (for which we *do* earn royalties, so if you want to support your favorite scholars, buy their books!). Most of these will be of interest to a very small audience. To be contented as an academic writer, one must accept a "fit audience, though few" and strive to do the work well, even if only a handful of people read it.

It's increasingly (although not universally) recognized that writing to a wider audience, making one's academic expertise accessible to the layperson, is a valuable skill for academics, so the life of a working academic writer today should include things like blog posts and articles for magazines and even, possibly, the occasional popular-level book. Even so, it's wise to keep in mind that writing is *work*. It's not a case of waiting for inspiration but of making time, day after day, year after year, to turn on your computer and—as the saying goes—apply the seat of the pants to the seat of the chair until you have produced a first draft. Then you need to get feedback, revise,

revise more, and send the pieces out into the world where much of the time they'll be rejected, and you'll need to learn from this and carry on.

Very few academics end up becoming public intellectuals, doing speaking engagements and media; this is the result of a narrow intersection of a person's skills, interests, and subject matter. Most academics present papers at conferences but will never give a public lecture. Many academics write blog posts and contribute articles to magazines about their subject but don't have a wider media reach. Keep in mind, as well, that when you see a video or read a book by a well-known academic, you can't see the years of labor in obscurity that provided the grounding to speak to a wider audience, or all the work that goes on day by day outside the limited light of the public sphere.

This picture of hard and often tedious (but good and fulfilling) work assumes that you've been able to *get* a job as an academic. The reality of academia at this present moment is that there are many more people who are highly qualified to be university or college professors than there are full-time jobs available.

One of the reasons for this is that most universities rely on graduate students to do a great deal of low-wage labor, teaching introductory classes and leading discussion sections. For many years, universities have thus had an incentive to admit more students to their doctoral programs than they could reasonably place in teaching jobs. Furthermore, some lower-profile universities have realized that they can gain prestige and tuition money through having PhD programs, in effect preying upon people with academic dreams. A degree from a university with a reputation for low-quality work by its graduates may be worse than having no PhD at all. A good program will be selective and will only admit those students who have the capacity to succeed and whose interests match up well with a specific supervisor; it will provide one-on-one faculty advising from the start; it will have faculty and alumni who regularly publish in reputable, relevant areas; it will be honest and forthright about job placement of graduates and ideally will provide career support post-graduation, whether for jobs in academia or outside it;

and it will be academically rigorous, which means that you can expect to find it tough going and that not everyone who is admitted will finish the degree. If it's quick and easy to get accepted and earn a PhD somewhere, run, don't walk, away from that program: it's setting you up to waste your time and money and hurt your future academic reputation and ability to get hired, for the vanity of having some letters after your name.

Another reason for the tight academic labor market is that colleges and universities increasingly rely on adjunct (part-time) faculty, who are paid by the class (and paid poorly), without benefits or job security; this is cheaper and easier for the universities but terrible for people caught in adjunct limbo. It's also bad for students, because faculty who have to juggle teaching assignments at multiple different colleges just to make ends meet won't have time for real mentoring or engagement with students. (Parents and prospective students: look carefully at a college's ratio of full-time to adjunct faculty and ask questions about who teaches the intro courses; colleges that rely heavily on adjunct faculty shouldn't be rewarded by receiving your tuition money.)

This is a grim picture, but it has to be faced. Earning a PhD or other advanced degree is grueling, and there's no guarantee of a job as a college professor at the end of it.

Thus far, all that I have said has been about the academic life in general and not directed specifically at women. That's mainly because one of the virtues of academia is that, at its best, it is a place where men and women can work on an equal footing, with equal respect, as colleagues in the academic enterprise. I have myself been fortunate in my academic career in that, in my graduate study in English literature, I had female professors, including my dissertation director, and in my work in the interdisciplinary field of C.S. Lewis, J.R.R. Tolkien, and the Inklings, there are many major scholars who are women. When I began to work in the field of apologetics, which is heavily male-dominated, I already had my PhD and a teaching career and could hold my own.

However—and here comes another bucket of cold water—women do face additional challenges in academia. To start with, sexual harassment is distressingly frequent and can come from female as well as male professors, supervisors, and fellow students. The same behavior from male or female students is sometimes viewed differently, as when speech that is positively "assertive" from a man is often considered negatively "aggressive" from a woman. In some Christian circles, the so-called "Billy Graham rule" (never being alone with a woman so as not to be tempted to have an affair) is crippling for women's academic and professional growth, as it hinders collegial conversations, collaborative work, mentoring, and simple friendship. (It's also demeaning to women, treating them first and foremost as objects of sexual attraction and denying agency to both men and women for their own behavior.)

Is "academia" a male space into which we are inserting ourselves, possibly as intruders? Many women find that "success" and "professionalism" in academia are sometimes framed such that it seems like we have to behave like men to be taken seriously. This can entail pressure to accept or even imitate male sexual misbehavior and vulgarity; to postpone or avoid having children, or to accept that spending time with one's children will hurt one's career; and more subtly, to conform to certain norms of appearance (such as the toxic idea that having curly hair demonstrates a lack of professionalism). There can also be conflicting social pressures, so that women in academia may feel that they are supposed to signal their femininity in specific ways, such as wearing high-heeled shoes and makeup.

It doesn't help matters that one's community outside academia might well believe that the academic life is unfeminine and should therefore be left to the men so that we women can follow more suitable, womanly pursuits. It is, in fact, absolutely possible to be a mother and an academic—I know many excellent scholars who are both—but women academics who have children face even more challenges with regard to conflicting and competing priorities and expectations. It can be a lonely life, being a woman in academia.

Now that you are, as it were, drenched and shivering with the cold water that I have thrown upon you, let me say that I am not suggesting the abandonment of the idea of academia, if that is your vocation. Rather, I am advocating a realistic view, one that allows you to make a wise decision, to count the costs, and to be prepared, if you go forward.

So far we have considered in detail the definition of academia as being "a member of a university or college's teaching or research staff." But that's not the whole picture. Remember that the OED notes that it is also "the academic community," and that an academic is "a person interested in or excelling at pursuits involving reading, thinking, and study."

If you want to be an academic, you will need to get some further education, but it need not be a PhD. A good master's degree is worthwhile for almost everyone and provides the foundation for scholarly work.

These days, an online master's can be as rigorous and valuable as a residential one and much more feasible for most people, but make sure that it fully measures up to a face-to-face program. If you get a sense that the online program is treated as an incidental add-on to the "real" residential program, run away! Whether online or in-person, look for a program where class sizes are small and the courses are taught by the major faculty (*not* by adjuncts or assistants). Make sure that the courses are rigorous, with plenty of primary-source reading and lots of writing or projects. Ask if the professors grade the papers for their own classes—this is probably the most revealing question for online programs—and if they don't, run away! Get in touch with professors in the program. Are they willing to talk to you beforehand? Consider the faculty roster as a lineup of potential academic mentors.

I encourage women to look for programs that have at least some women faculty and a decent number of women students. You may well find that your main mentors and collaborators end up being men, depending on the match-up of personality, interests, and aptitudes, but it is encouraging to be in an environment in which there are other women working alongside you.

Then do the work: attend academic conferences and present papers at them; write book reviews for journals in your field; write blog posts, essays, and book chapters; teach as and when you can; and see where, in God's providence, you end up. It may be that you'll find yourself increasingly drawn to advanced graduate study, and if so, you can take that step knowing more fully what challenges are ahead. It may be that you'll find—as many have—a rich and fruitful academic life, a teaching career, perhaps a writing or editing career, right where you are.

To be an academic is, in my view, to love the life of the mind and to be committed to doing the work of scholarship in whatever field you find yourself most deeply invested in. It is a vocation. If you feel this call to a lifetime of scholarly work, of writing and teaching, you might eventually earn an advanced degree and seek to become a college professor. But it is not "all or nothing." Set aside the rose-tinted glasses and look at it this way: Do you want to be a scholar? Then *do the work*, and strive for excellence in all that you do.

Read widely and deeply, with attention and care, with discipline and reflection. Learn to write well and clearly, with precision and without jargon; learn the language and style of your discipline. This will help you to discern if you love academia as a place to do your life's work or if you are merely attracted to the *idea* of academia, the "Oxford Disneyland" mirage. Writers write; researchers research; scholars do scholarly reading. If you actually *find the time* to do the work (not repeating the refrain of "if I had time" or "one day"), and you discover that *doing* those things (not just imagining yourself as a person who does these things) energizes and sustains you, then you are well on your way toward being part of the academic community.

This is the academic life: to do the work of scholarship, to be part of a community of scholars, to be engaged in a life of reading, thinking, and study—and all the hard work that entails. It is a world where both the feminine and the masculine intellect are equal, valued, and necessary. And it can be, and often is, deeply rewarding.

It is rewarding to research a topic deeply and achieve mastery of a given field. It is rewarding to see one's ideas being taken seriously and contributing to one's area of expertise. It is rewarding to earn royalties from publications and honoraria from public speaking. Perhaps most rewarding of all is to see former students and mentees doing good work of their own out there in the world. For example, a few years ago, a group of my former students from

Houston Baptist University's MA in Apologetics program founded a peer-reviewed journal of cultural apologetics called *An Unexpected Journal*, an endeavor that is going strong. In one sense, this journal was "unexpected" by me, in that one never knows precisely where one's influence will bear particular fruit. But in another more general sense, this sort of thing is indeed to be expected. If one's expectations are realistic about the debit side of the academic life, one can also legitimately expect many positives on the credit side of the ledger, many of them surprising, delightful, and exciting. They make the academic life a joy, one which I am profoundly grateful for and cannot imagine my life without.

The Mind of Writing

Tsh Oxenreider

I was plagued with postpartum depression when I was in the early days of motherhood. I didn't know it at the time; as a newcomer to the vocation, I assumed my experience was part and parcel of the gig. It wasn't until two years later, sitting on a therapist's couch with a box of tissues in one hand and my husband's hand in the other, that I discovered that how I felt about motherhood, deep down, wasn't the expectation nor the state of mind I'd have to assume for the rest of my life (considering I was also pregnant with our next baby). My methods and rhythms of mothering would, indeed, change as my kids changed from newborns to adults, and I was not doomed to diapers and toddler tantrums for all eternity. I knew this, rationally, but my soul still needed the clarification. I needed help seeing the light at the end of the early motherhood tunnel.

God bless this therapist because, in addition to medication, regular therapy, and a few other practical prescriptions to my daily modus operandi, he also suggested I find a hobby. And though I should have been grateful, gratitude was *not* my immediate reaction when he recommended I combat depression with some kind of leisure activity. Pursuing a hobby with a toddler on my hip and a pre-born curled in my abdomen was as appealing as holding an in-depth reading of Shakespeare for my dog. My entire life was eating, feeding others, finding sleep in the nooks and crannies of spare time, and occasionally treating myself to the luxury of a ten-minute shower. Rinse and repeat, day after day. Pursuing a hobby was so far down the list of things to do that I couldn't see it if I squinted. I knew not the definition of the word.

As we pulled out of his office parking lot, my husband turned left toward a café for our lunch date and said, nonchalantly, "What about writing?"

"What do you mean?" I asked.

"For your hobby. You've always liked to write. Could be good for you."

"I don't think so. Is writing a hobby?"

"Anything can be a hobby."

I sat there, quiet. Could *anything* be a hobby? When I first heard the therapist's suggestion, I pictured a brightly colored kayak on the bay near our apartment or some sort of local painting class or an intramural sports team. And I had no interest in pursuing any of those things.

"Look, writing is good," he continued. "You can do it from anywhere and it's nearly free to start one of those blogs. I could see you doing it."

"Huh," was my lofty, maundering response.

It took a few months, but one Sunday afternoon while my newly born son slept, I opened a blank doc and stared at the blinking cursor that was daring me to say something. It felt like I had nothing to say, but I desperately wanted to say something, anything. Turns out I was both right and wrong—because I had nothing to say until I started saying it. Stringing a few words together into sentences revealed to me that I did, in fact, have an idea or two; ideas I didn't even know existed. Depression fogged my brain and taped shut my mouth, which meant it was hard both to think cogently and to speak with clarity. But writing—writing my thoughts gave me a sliver of space to recognize the woman still inside, hiding somewhere beneath the murk and mire of parenting babies.

I wrote small at first: a hack I just learned about loading silverware in the dishwasher, how I sewed reusable shopping bags out of old T-shirts. But then I started penning a few thoughts that frightened me to come into existence. Writing them down, even digitally, made them more real: that I wished we lived in a house instead of an apartment, that even though she was only three I was already sad about my daughter one day leaving the house. I dared to write about how I couldn't hear God's voice. I took a cue from David the king and wrote a frustrated poem to my depression.

Something strange happened, though. Writing down real thoughts, sculpting them from shapeless clay into tailored ideas, actually made them less scary, not more. My voice was given a microphone, even if it was tiny and just for me and a few readers, and I discovered I quite liked the sound of me exercising my agency. Making space for my words cleared space in my mind, which breathed much-needed life into my soul. I became more present in my daily life. I became more myself.

Several pregnancies, five houses, and thousands of miles of travel later, I can sit at this unimpressive kitchen table a continent away from that first nudge toward a writing life, take another sip of my morning coffee, stare at the decaying marigolds in the mason jar next to me, and say without hesitation, "God bless that therapist."

My armory was full of weapons at my disposal to massacre the demon of depression when it reared its ugly head, but the craft of writing became the knife I sharpened near daily. It sliced through the fog of motherhood, yes, but it also kept at bay weeds of doubt, confusion, passivity, and reticence when they crept through the soil. Writing provided a voice my introverted soul needed. It clarified my beliefs when I wasn't sure what I thought about cloth diapers, the best method of spring cleaning, the real presence in the Eucharist, or the intersection of childhood education with the philosophy of Josef Pieper. It helped me unearth poetry found in the backyard tomato crop. It quieted the brain rattle. It warded off the demons of doubt and despair, cousins of my depression. Writing made me brave from my kitchen table.

Writing has made me a better wife and mom. It has made me a better woman.

It's been widely said that writing is a form of thinking. The science backs this up, as does my own personal experience and the hearsay of many more folks who consider themselves the writing sort. A blank journal page and pen or the blinking cursor on a white screen serve as a canvas on which to slather different colors of ideas. When I find myself unsure of how to understand a statement made in my priest's latest homily or stuck on how to make my next subtle move in the delicate dance of parenting teens, stitching letters together to form words, then sentences, then ultimately ideas often serves as my primary brain decoder. The mere act of scribbling out my thoughts, haphazard or contradictory though they may be, breathes them into life on paper. They become real. They no longer live as nonexistent particles floating around in my mind; in no small way is thinking by writing akin to giving birth and creating life. Thinking by writing gives ideas sentience.

Even if it's a terrible idea, the Frankenstein behind the prolix monster could technically point to the jumble of words and say, "There, over there. I made that. That's a thing I did." It might very well deserve a funeral pyre, of course, but for just a few seconds, it inhaled and exhaled. Several monsters later, a decent idea may very well stand up with symmetrical features and cogent qualities and take a few toddled steps on its own. But it never would have had the chance at life were it not for the wordsmith tinkering in the lab in the first place.

Women benefit from being these wordsmiths. Writing, big or small but nonetheless with intention, gives us space to think lucidly. When we write, we untangle our mess of thoughts—even if it's only for a minute, even if it's only about one thing—and we set down the pen more clearheaded. We are more apt to be out and about in the world with a sliver more clarity about some of life's true conundrums: *Why does God permit so much pain in the world? Why do waves move in tandem with the moon? Why are we the way that we are? How do watches work?*

We may not close the journal as experts, but we have tangible proof that we've contemplated an idea, and we leave the pages between the covers half-a-percent wiser than when we started, even if the wisdom gained is a deeper realization of how little we know about the mystery of the world (perhaps especially when that happens).

And what a gain to our neighborhoods, dinner tables, office hours, and rocking chairs when a woman grows in wisdom! What a benefit to our own peace of mind when we're folding towels and reconciling budgets and we know just a bit more about God's unfathomable world. How much our character deepens when we grow in wisdom, no matter what life stage we're in. Writing grows our character.

Writing also enriches our imaginations. Putting pen to paper shapes entirely new things out of near-nothing: heroes, villains, settings, conflicts, dialogue—the ingredients in a story, that most human of innovative things.

I was nursing my third-born when I finally read the Harry Potter series, and I bawled like the baby in my arms when Dumbledore called Harry a man in the heaven-like King's Cross Station near the end. The thought of a nothing-orphan in the first book maturing closer to manhood by the seventh infused more hope in me that my own children may one day grow in grit through life's challenges. It gave me hope that I would too.

This is reading, of course, and not writing, and I could share similar anecdotes with even more conviction about Tolkien's lore, Chesterton's mysteries, and L'Engle's distant planets. But writing is reading's companion, another side of the same coin, and writing tales enriches our visits to other writers' imaginative worlds.

It's easy to brush ourselves off as unimaginative; "I'm not creative" is the whimpering battle cry of far too many women. To create, though, is to be human at our very core; our nature is that of a creator because we're creatures made in the likeness of God, the ultimate Maker. When we create, we tap into the divine likeness God poured into us when he saw it fit to make us in his own image. Creating might mean the literal creation of new life, but it could also be through a medium like writing or painting or composing or gardening, or through the simple act of recapping a childhood story over drinks with a neighbor friend. Storytelling is perhaps one of our oldest human endeavors in creating like our Creator, and we do it all the time. Sometimes, we do it on paper.

Imagine the worlds our own world would be bereft of without the tenacity of women to pen them: Anne's Avonlea on Prince Edward Island, the March sisters' boisterous living room, the Gryffindor common room, Jane's wild English moors north of Thornfield Hall, Janie Crawford's mucky

Florida everglades, your own imaginative world you escape to as a balm when the real world asks so much of you.

The doggedness of writing makes women deeper thinkers and more imaginative storytellers, yet it also serves the world with a practical purpose: it passes down her culture. It's been said that the primary, noblest purpose of education is to pass culture down to the next generation, and I'm inclined to agree. Whatever we find most necessary for life on earth, our species' survival depends on teaching our children how to survive and thrive. *This is how to feed yourself, this is how to change a flat tire, this is the Pythagorean Theorem.* Much of our culture is, in fact, our culture because it was preserved through writing. Think of where we might be without the 1,700 words invented by Shakespeare, without the scribbled notes for Bach's *St. Matthew Passion*, or without Julia Child's art of proletarian French cooking.

Yet what about the pound cake recipe from *your* own grandmother? The stories of your great-aunt's brother-in-law's grandmother who changed the trajectory of your family tree? What it means to be someone with your last name out in the world, spending your days as a neighbor and friend? Which music mattered most deeply at the height of your parents' teen years?

We could get lost in the curiosity of what stories we've missed in the dust of fleeting time because someone didn't bother to write them down. There are billions of them. Most we'll never know this side of heaven—and yet there are a few that have stayed. The ones we decided were worth spilling ink on paper for are the ones that we leaf through in the tomes on bookstore shelves and read through greased pencil smudges on family heirloom recipe cards.

A few women should feel compelled to write so that others can visit their inventions and imaginative worlds. Even more women should want to write to deepen their own wisdom, enriching their core humanness and becoming more virtuous in the process. Yet I hope that many, many more women choose to pick up a pen so that their own lores aren't forgotten. Our world *needs* their computer coding, their mathematical theories, their maternal wisdom, their poetry, their sci-fis and whodunnits, and their green bean casseroles.

Women should write because writing makes us more human, and women should write because it makes the world better. But where to begin? How, in the midst of ordinary modern life, does the average ordinary woman find time and space to write?

It sounds trite, but the first place to begin is with pen and paper. Its simplicity is almost laughable. Any ten-cent spiral notebook will do, but it's also often a worthwhile ceremony to buy a new journal in a favorite color and pair it with a smooth-gliding pen. The point is to make writing accessible, so whatever the tools, the beginning step is to make them handy. Lessen the friction of writing by keeping a notebook and pen at easy reach. I like to keep my softcover Leuchtturm 1917 dotted journal at home base by my nightstand lamp, with a zebra ballpoint pen twisted in its elastic strap.

Then, write.

I tell my high school students that the point is to keep the pen moving, not to assume the endeavor will reveal your hidden calling as the next Austen. In fact, it's prudent to assume your first scribbles won't be very good. Writing is like turning on an old tap: you have to let the rusty water flow out first before it becomes clear.

Even our abominable writing is educational, however, because it teaches us the art of patience, the habit of thinking clearly and deeply, and the power of draining out that rusty water. What is a great way to let out the bad writing and transform it into succinct, thoughtful writing? A time-tested practice called freewriting. It's a vehicle by which we trick ourselves into divesting the words and ideas we want to share but are afraid won't come out "right" on paper. The freedom to make mistakes, safely explore thoughts and ideas, and focus on what we want to say more than how we're going to say it makes us more comfortable, courageous, and compelling writers.

If you're not sure where to begin, start with gratitude. After your morning alarm rings (be it the backyard rooster, the baby, the vibration of your smartwatch, or if you're truly blessed, the sun), wipe the sleep from your eyes and jot down three specific things you're thankful for. They may be deeply theological, but it's not necessary—a mix of gratitude for both the Immaculate Conception and the high-quality roast of beans in a mug is frequently comforting. Over time, your eclectic list of gratitude will serve as something your descendants can mark as family history.

The greatest writers also know how to steal like an artist, so follow suit and follow their absconding ways. Keep a commonplace book and gather a collection of your favorite quotations from other writers. In medieval times, commonplace books were called *florilegium*, a portmanteau of the Latin words *flos* (flower) and *legere* (to gather): literally, a gathering of flowers. A bouquet! Wordsmith your way with a posy arrangement of well-said words that reflect the working of your own mind. Deep and shallow pair just fine together; my commonplace book is a healthy mix of St. John Henry Newman and Michael Scott.

The act of written gratitude and common-placing might be enough for a busy woman, and these practices are indeed sufficient: these two virtuous endeavors already leave a paper trail to your enriched inner life. But they might further spur you on to moving that blinking cursor and drafting a few thoughts about what it means to love like Samwise, or perhaps how it feels to apply, boots on the ground, Aquinas' definition of love to your childhood friend. You might unearth an opinion you never knew you had about foreign policy. Your *florilegia* could perhaps lead you to discover a Middle-earth of your own invention that you can't help but give birth to with a pen. And oh, how our world *needs* your world.

Perchance you could even take, with modest sagacity, the blazing torch passed down from the lettered women in our great cloud of witnesses: Flannery O'Connor, St. Catherine of Siena, St. Edith Stein, St. Teresa of Avila. These women wrote in spite of themselves. They wrote because God gave them a pen. They gave birth to paragraphs, and our world changed for the better because of it. You need not be them. You need simply be you. But what great company you'll be in when you write.

Fundamentally, we write because God whispers in our ears and we want to respond in kind to the world. As Madeleine L'Engle once said in *Walking on Water*, "To work on a book is for me very much the same thing as to pray. . . . Ultimately, when you are writing, you stop thinking and write what you hear."[1]

The strength of women is stamped and cataloged by their words, and their words illuminate the voice of God. We're gifted with the gift of giving birth to new life.

God speaks to women. Women deliver into the world these words when they write.

God speaks to you. Perhaps you're compelled to give life to this on paper.

---

1. Madeleine L'Engle, *Walking on Water: Reflections on Faith and Art* (New York: Convergent Books, 2016), 140.

Contributors

Amanda Achtman is pursuing a degree in Judaic Studies and Jewish-Christian Relations at the Pontifical Gregorian University in Rome. She recently served as the Senior Advisor to a Canadian parliamentarian, working to prevent the expansion of euthanasia to persons living with a disability or mental illness.

Jackie Francois Angel is the Pope St. Paul VI Fellow of Marriage and Family Life at the Word on Fire Institute. Hailing from Orange County, CA, she is a speaker, vlogger, author, and singer-songwriter. In 2006, she was signed to Spirit & Song, a division of OCP, and she debuted her first album, *Your Kingdom Is Glorious*, in 2008. Her sophomore album, *Divine Comedy*, was released in 2012. Along with being a blogger and webcast host, Jackie travels around the world speaking, singing, sampling the local cuisine, and attempting to make people laugh. In 2013, Jackie married Bobby Angel, who shares her passion for Jesus, coffee, and superhero movies. They reside in North Texas with their four young children.

Rachel Bulman is the editor of this volume. She is a lover of humanity, especially her husband and six children. Rachel will soon be releasing her first book, *Becoming Wife: Self-Gift in Matrimony*, and is currently working on her next book. She has written and hosted a television series for Catholic TV about Eucharistic miracles. She appears with her family in the show *Meet the Bulmans* currently airing on the Word on Fire Institute's YouTube channel. She serves on the advisory board of The GIVEN Institute and frequently gives talks at retreats, conferences, and other gatherings. In her spare time, she enjoys reading a good book, lifting weights, and perfecting her old-fashioned cocktail recipe.

Emily Stimpson Chapman is an award-winning Catholic writer based in Pittsburgh, Pennsylvania. She is the author of six books, including most recently *Letters to Myself from the End of the World, Hope to Die: The Christian Meaning of Death and the Resurrection of the Body* (co-authored with Scott Hahn), and *The Catholic Table: Finding Joy Where Food and Faith Meet*. She has also authored six studies for the women's ministry Endow, is the editor and co-author of the *Formed in Christ* high school textbook series, and is the author of numerous Bible studies, as well as articles and essays for Catholic publications. Honored by both the Catholic Media Association and the Associated Church Press, Chapman lives in Pittsburgh with her husband and three young children.

Stephanie Gray Connors has given more than one thousand pro-life presentations and debates over two decades in ten countries, including speaking on abortion at Google headquarters and debating in Mexico at La Ciudad de las Ideas (CDI), an event similar to TED Talks. She holds a Bachelor of Arts in political science from UBC in Vancouver and a Certification with Distinction in health care ethics from the National Catholic Bioethics Center in Philadelphia. Stephanie has authored pro-life apologetics books on the beginning and end of life and blogs over at www.loveunleasheslife.com.

Jennifer Frey, PhD, is Associate Professor of Philosophy at the University of South Carolina and Fellow of the Institute for Human Ecology at the Catholic University of America. She has written numerous academic essays on virtue and human agency, has edited three books, and frequently writes and lectures for non-academic audiences. She is also the host of the literature, philosophy, and theology podcast titled *Sacred and Profane Love*.

123

Sr. Josephine Garrett, CSFN, is a sister of the Holy Family of Nazareth. Her community's mission is to help spread the kingdom of God's love in the world especially through ministry to families. She currently lives in Tyler, Texas, and serves families as a school counselor and as a clinical mental health counselor in a private practice. She has also served as a national speaker and writer for many Catholic ministries.

Rachel Harkins Ullmann serves as the Executive Director of The GIVEN Institute. She is a graduate of Franciscan University of Steubenville, where she majored in theology and catechetics, and she later obtained her master's degree in education administration from Johns Hopkins University. Rachel is a harpist and has traveled to Australia, Israel, and all over Europe (favorite cities being Rome and Lourdes). Her greatest sources of joy are her husband, Tony, and her children, Evangeline, Cooper, and Theodore.

Sr. Miriam James Heidland, SOLT, is a member of the Society of Our Lady of the Most Holy Trinity. She is the author of two books and speaks extensively across the nation on the topics of healing, forgiveness, and authentic love.

Meg Hunter-Kilmer is an itinerant missionary and storyteller who travels the world telling people about the fierce and tender love of God. You can read more of her work in *Saints Around the World* (an international saint storybook for children) or *Pray for Us: 75 Saints Who Sinned, Suffered, and Struggled on Their Way to Holiness*.

Sr. Theresa Aletheia Noble, FSP, is a religious sister with the Daughters of St. Paul, a congregation founded by Blessed James Alberione to spread the Gospel using modern media. She is the author of several books on *memento mori*, the Christian practice of meditating on one's death to prepare for heaven. You can find out more about her ministry at pursuedbytruth.com.

Holly Ordway is the Cardinal Francis George Fellow of Faith and Culture at the Word on Fire Institute and Visiting Professor of Apologetics at Houston Baptist University. She holds a PhD in English from the University of Massachusetts Amherst and is the author of *Tolkien's Modern Reading: Middle-earth Beyond the Middle Ages* and *Apologetics and the Christian Imagination: An Integrated Approach to Defending the Faith*, as well as co-editor of the Word on Fire Classics volume the *Ignatian Collection*. She is also a Subject Editor for the *Journal of Inklings Studies* and a published poet.

Tsh Oxenreider is the author of several books, including the liturgical guides *Bitter & Sweet* for Lent and *Shadow & Light* for Advent, as well as *At Home in the World*, the story of her family's year traveling around the world out of backpacks. She's also a podcaster, writes a long-running newsletter, leads pilgrimages, teaches high school, and helps people create their rules of life. Learn more at tshoxenreider.com.

Leah Libresco Sargeant is the author of *Arriving at Amen* and *Building the Benedict Option*. She runs Other Feminisms, a Substack community.

Elizabeth Scalia, OblOSB, is Editor-at-Large at the Word on Fire Institute and the author of several award-winning books, including *Strange Gods* and *Little Sins Mean a Lot*.

Susanna Spencer is a homeschooling mother of four and lives with her husband and family in St. Paul, Minnesota. She holds a master's degree in theology from Franciscan University of Steubenville and is a writer and theological editor for Blessed is She, narrator of the children's devotional book *Rise Up: Shining with Virtue*, and regular contributor to the *National Catholic Register*.

Contributors

Haley Stewart is the Managing Editor of Word on Fire Spark. She co-hosts *The Fountains of Carrots Podcast* and is the author of *The Grace of Enough, Jane Austen's Genius Guide to Life,* and a series for young readers titled *The Sister Seraphina Mysteries.* Haley and her husband have four children.